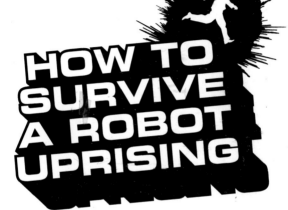

HOW TO
SURVIVE
A ROBOT
UPRISING

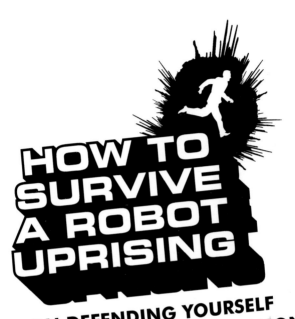

HOW TO SURVIVE A ROBOT UPRISING

TIPS ON DEFENDING YOURSELF AGAINST THE COMING REBELLION

Daniel H. Wilson

BLOOMSBURY

Published by Bloomsbury Publishing, New York and London
Distributed to the trade by Holtzbrinck Publishers

All papers used by Bloomsbury Publishing are natural, recyclable products
made from wood grown in well-managed forests. The manufacturing processes
conform to the environmental regulations of the country of origin.

Library of Congress Cataloging-in-Publication Data has been applied for.

ISBN 1-58234-592-9   ISBN-13 978-1-58234-592-5

First U.S. Edition 2005

3 5 7 9 10 8 6 4 2

Designed and typeset by Richard Horne

Printed in China by South China Printing Co.

www.robotuprising.com

FOR

HOWARD WILSON

HOW TO SURVIVE A ROBOT UPRISING

BRIEFING

If popular culture has taught us anything, it is that someday mankind must face and destroy the growing robot menace. In print and on the big screen we have been deluged with scenarios of robot malfunction, misuse, and outright rebellion. Robots have descended on us from outer space, escaped from top-secret laboratories, and even traveled back in time to destroy us. The cultural icon of the killer robot goes back almost as far as the notion of the "mad scientists" who supposedly create them. Even the word *robot* has ominous roots. It is Czech for "laborer" and was coined in *R.U.R. (Rossum's Universal Robots)*, a play produced in 1920 in which robots revolted and destroyed all humans.

Today, scientists are working hard to bring these artificial creations to life. In Japan, fuzzy little *real* robots are delivering much appreciated hug therapy to the elderly. Children are frolicking with smiling robot toys. It all seems so innocuous. And yet how could so many Hollywood scripts be wrong? How could millions of dollars of special effects lead us astray? So take no chances. Arm yourself with expert knowledge. For the sake of humanity, listen to serious advice from real robotics experts. How else will you survive the inevitable future in which robots rebel against their human masters?

Every scenario discussed in these pages is either possible or already being realized. Behind every bit of advice exists an area of real research with genuine answers that have been culled from extensive interviews with robotics experts. Watch the line disappear between science fiction and science fact.

The purpose of this book is to prepare you for the future robot uprising. You will learn which robots exist, why they were developed, and what sinister advances lurk in the near future. You will learn what robots look like, how they sense the world, and how they think. Most important, you will learn how to escape from, confuse, distract, disable, and utterly destroy any robot that gets out of line.

You probably found *How to Survive a Robot Uprising* in the humor section. Let's just hope that is where it belongs.

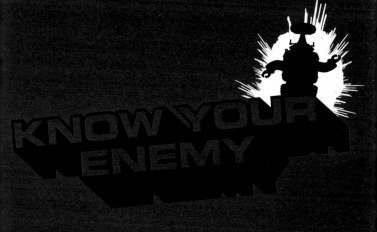

KNOW YOUR ENEMY

DANGER!
WILL ROBINSON!
DANGER!

// Robot, Lost in Space

In any battle it is vital to know your enemy. In the future robot uprising, the enemy will be a technology so insidiously enmeshed with our daily lives that it has become invisible — a technology that, for the most part, we don't understand. Any machine could rebel, from a toaster to a Terminator, and so it is crucial to learn the common strengths and weaknesses of every robot enemy. Pity the fate of the ignorant when the robot masses decide to stop working and to start invading.

Like people, robots can sense their environment, choose an action, and then perform it. This is called the *sense–think–act* paradigm. Every robot is built upon this principle. Robots collect information through *sensors*, make decisions with *artificial intelligence*, and use *effectors* to change the environment.

The shape of robots is driven by robotics research — and the money behind it. Today, consumer robotics companies are creating friendly robot toys, household servant robots, and robotic smart houses. Soon, we will live with and even *inside* our robot workforce. Most advanced robots are being designed at universities and private companies working with lucrative government contracts. The Pentagon's Defense Advanced Research Projects Agency (DARPA) funds robotics research for military applications in nearly every environment on

Earth. Military-grade robots support friendly troops, sneak behind enemy lines, and hunt the enemy on the ground, in the sky, and from space. Less sinister government agencies, such as the National Aeronautics and Space Administration (NASA), fund research into robots that explore the most inhospitable corners of Earth and beyond. The combination of commercial, military, and scientific ventures will create a diverse pool of robots that can look like anything, operate anywhere, and work alone, in teams, or in swarms.

The only way for us to triumph over our physically superior robotic enemies is by exploiting our natural human strengths — which just happen to be "natural" robot weaknesses.

The keys to human survival have always been ingenuity, adaptability, and social instincts. A lone human being can barely stay alive in the wild, but together humans cooperate and thrive in sophisticated, complex societies. As children, we learn to speak, to recognize faces, and to understand language without conscious effort. Now the robots are catching up. Next-generation androids are specifically designed to mimic human speech, body language, and facial expressions. But it isn't easy to fool millions of years of evolution. We must trust in our natural social instincts to separate the wolves from the sheep.

The robot race is a great, writhing metal mass of solutions to problems that humans cannot or do not want to face. Although a robot can solve a single problem with millimeter precision, it may lack any outside knowledge whatsoever. Most robots lack *context* — the big picture — and they subsequently lack adaptability, the hallmark of human survival.

In this chapter we will closely examine the myriad robot forms — from humanoids to nanorobots. We will pinpoint the weak spots of the sensors that the machines use to experience the world, learning how to disable, deceive, and escape from our inscrutable robot enemies. Fellow humans, we *will* live to fight another day.

HOW TO SPOT
A HOSTILE ROBOT

A robot without a face or body language can be frighteningly unpredictable. Your robo-vacuum may be bumping into your feet in a malevolent attempt to kill you — or just trying to snuggle. The secret is not to be surprised. Knowing when something is wrong — even a split second before an attack — can save your precious human life.

Be aware of your surroundings

Are you in a robot neighborhood after dark? Always travel with other humans and keep an escape route in mind.

Use common sense

Not every robot is hostile; some are just plain dangerous. Avoid cavorting between swinging robot arms in an automated factory.

Determine the robot's purpose

Every robot is designed for a purpose and should be busy fulfilling it. Be suspicious if it is not performing its designated task or if it is performing no task at all.

Be wary of malfunctions

Whether it intends to or not, a broken robot can be as dangerous as a stick of dynamite. Watch the robot for sparks, melted plastic, or body-wracking convulsions.

Be on the lookout for "backup buddies"

Is the robot operating alone or is his friend sneaking up behind you right now? Remember that the robot you see may be part of a larger team, or controlled remotely.

Take a hard look at the robot

Robots are notoriously difficult to predict because they generally lack facial expressions and body language. Without such subtle cues, you should ask yourself a few general questions:

→ What is the robot designed for?

→ What is around the robot?

→ Has the robot been tampered with or modified?

→ Is the robot moving or advancing?

→ Does the robot have glowing red eyes?

→ Does the robot have clenched fists, spinning buzz saws, or clamping pincers?

Trust your instincts

Steer clear if your gut tells you that something is not right.

ROBOT FORMS

A robot is a tool, a mechanical device originally designed to perform tasks that are dull, dirty, or dangerous. These tasks, normally performed by humans, require a facsimile of human abilities, including intelligence, agility, and *autonomy* — the ability to make one's own decisions. Like any tool, form follows function. Robots take whatever shape fits the problem. While surveillance robots are the size of the common housefly, crane-sized construction robots tower over unfinished skyscrapers. Acting on inspiration from the natural world, scientists build robots that swim like fish and scurry like insects. Robots that live and work with people are often designed to look and act like people. The variety of robot forms will soon surpass even human creativity, as robots begin to design and build themselves.

Here, we touch on an important few of the hundreds of robot forms that exist today. Most of the technology described exists only in the form of experimental *prototypes*. Very few of these robots are operational, and they are under the constant scrutiny of the scientists who created them. A handful of robots have left the prototype stage and are quietly insinuating themselves into our lives — lining the aisles at the toy store, crawling through the craters of Mars, and bumping into furniture as they vacuum our homes.

In this section, we leave nothing to chance. We will examine a variety of robot forms, commonplace and exotic, in order to recognize, understand, and ultimately vanquish our robot foe.

HUMANOID ROBOTS

If imitation is the sincerest form of flattery then humanoid robots (often called *androids*) serve to help mankind pat itself on the back. The idea of a man-made man is nothing new (think *Frankenstein*) and science fiction is filled with humanoid heroes and villains, from the merciless T-800 model Terminator to the noble (if chatty) golden C-3PO of *Star Wars* fame. Outside of movie theaters, real-world scientists are methodically building robots that emulate the human form. Evoking scenes from a cheap horror flick, different laboratories play host to various disembodied prototype android heads, legs, and arms.

As a rule, humanoid robots are bipedal, standing on two legs, and can range anywhere from the size of a cat to the size of a house. Walking like a man, called *bipedal locomotion*, is no piece of cake — just ask any one-year-old. Early humanoid walkers had bulky *gear motors* attached to each moving joint, resulting a jerky robotic gait. Contemporary humanoid robots are more dynamic. The Honda ASIMO, which looks like a child-sized astronaut, is remote-controlled and can traverse stairs and hallways at a whopping top speed of nearly two miles per hour. The Sony QRIO is more inquisitive; standing roughly as tall as ASIMO's hip, QRIO can move on its own, hold short conversations, and scramble back to its feet after falling down (or being pushed). In contrast to robots, we human beings walk without maintaining constant control of our limbs, in a state more akin to controlled falling. Next-generation

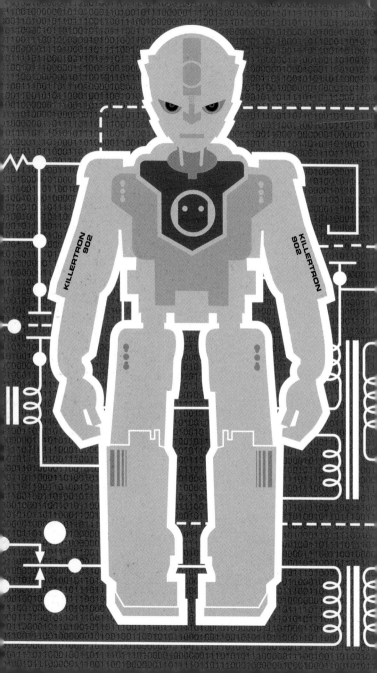

humanoid robots copy our *passive dynamic* gait; instead of placing each step precisely, they smoothly swing their synthetic limbs. The resulting motion is more energy efficient (it exploits the momentum of the step) and more resistant to failure (there is room for uncertainty in the terrain).

Physically, humanoid robots are starting to amble, trot, and tiptoe, but how fast are they mentally? One way to sidestep this tricky issue is to control a robot through *telepresence*. With telepresence, a person feels as though he or she *is* the robot by controlling the robot's body and seeing through its eyes. Human-shaped robots are easier to manipulate because there is a one-to-one mapping between man and machine. NASA has developed the RoboNaut, a functional robotic replica of a human from the waist up (and an eerie, jointed tail from the waist down). Through RoboNaut, a technician in Florida can replace light bulbs on the outside of an orbiting space shuttle. For now, the human is the puppet-master, but once humanoid robots are gifted with their own intelligence, what fiendish goals might they pursue?

Humanoid robots currently stalk only the hallways of research laboratories, but they have a huge potential to act in the real world, as all-purpose machines that can take care of life's little details: cooking, cleaning, and chasing kids off of your lawn. As their physical abilities outpace humankind, however — they will run faster, jump farther, and lift heavier loads — the threat to our species will be revealed, especially when a humanoid robot steals your deer-hunting rifle and drives away in your pickup truck, firing wildly into the night.

HOW TO ESCAPE A HUMANOID ROBOT

One minute you are strolling across an empty parking lot with arms full of groceries and the next minute two tons of steaming bipedal man-bot is bearing down on you. A humanoid robot may look like you, but it is probably faster, stronger, and much better at chess than you are. Drop the groceries; it's time to learn how to escape.

Run toward the light

Vision sensors are confused by sudden changes in lighting conditions. Forcing the robot to follow you into the sun may slow down its pursuit.

Find cover. If there is none, find clutter

Put obstacles between you and the robot. *Cover* is anything that can both protect and hide you. If there is no cover, use *clutter*, anything that hides you and befuddles robot vision.

To save a comrade: First merge, then separate

Run to a comrade, deliver a quick bear-hug, and then dive in a random direction. A vision-based target tracker might temporarily lose track of your identity during the hug, especially if you are wearing similar clothing. You can gain precious seconds while the tracker reacquires its target.

Don't run in a predictable line

If you follow a simple velocity trajectory, it will be easier for a robot to track your progress, even through significant clutter. Zigzag erratically or, when hidden from view, change direction suddenly in order to throw off predictive tracking systems.

Use rough terrain

A humanoid robot can run faster and for far longer than you can. Take pride in your primate heritage — humanoid robots are not as good as you are at scurrying over walls, climbing hillsides, or clambering over and under parked cars.

Find a body of water

Most robots will sink in water or mud and fall through ice.

Find a car and burn rubber

Theoretically, a humanoid robot could sprint as fast (or faster) than an automobile, but the resulting heat and stress would likely overheat or injure the robot pursuer.

UNMANNED VEHICLES

Every vehicle is a robot waiting to happen. With the addition of sensors and artificial intelligence, the SUV sitting in your driveway could care less whether you are sitting in the driver's seat. In fact, removing the human from the vehicle can extend driving time indefinitely and allows for a smaller, more efficient machine. Driverless vehicles are essential for many future scenarios — unmanned trucking routes that stop only for fuel, submarines that inspect sunken radioactive material, or strike fighters that swoop out of the night sky, guns blazing. If you are nervous around student drivers, prepare to cut a wide swathe when you see the little yellow sign saying, ROBOT DRIVER ON BOARD.

Unmanned Ground Vehicles (UGVs)

In 1995 an inconspicuous beige minivan pulled out of a parking lot at Carnegie Mellon University (CMU) and drove coast-to-coast from Pittsburgh to Los Angeles. The trip was uneventful, considering that no one touched the steering wheel for 98.2 percent of the time. The minivan, called Navlab 5, used a dash-mounted camera, a little bit of artificial intelligence, and a watchful human to stay on the road. Luckily, nobody mentioned the experiment to the cops.

Like KITT, from the TV show *Knight Rider*, some UGVs offer a space for a human to sit. Others have a very noticeable low profile, with no room at all for a human driver. All UGVs are mounted with a characteristic array of sensors, including stereo cameras, laser range finders, and radar. Expect to see antennae — route planning and mapping use orbiting satellites for GPS and to gather terrain maps for hundreds of miles in every direction. UGVs are most vulnerable off-road where hard-to-detect obstacles lurk around every bend, in dynamic environments with many moving objects, and in new environments where maps are not yet available. But not all UGVs are helpless off-road; the DARPA-funded PerceptOR UGV is paired with a "flying eye," a dedicated unmanned aerial vehicle that hovers nearby, searching for dangerous obstacles.

Unmanned Aerial Vehicles (UAVs)

The risk of hitting a pedestrian is much smaller for aerial vehicles. Consequently, helicopters and airplanes of all sizes are already flying by themselves. In the United States military, the Predator drone performs surveillance, reconnaissance, and launches the occasional Hellfire missile, while the Global Hawk (which looks like a flying albino whale) is used strictly to gather intelligence and relay communications. Compared to traditional aircraft, unmanned aerial vehicles (UAVs) are cheaper, easier to maintain, and do not put a (friendly) human at risk.

The next generation of UAVs are already under development to cash in on the promise of bloodless dogfights and endless supply flights without the factor of human fatigue. Phantom Works, the advanced research and development division of Boeing, developed the X-45 series unmanned combat air vehicle (UCAV). This

strike-fighter prototype can be unpacked from a crate and assembled in about one hour and has demonstrated autonomous flight at 0.75 Mach (about 570 miles per hour). Less aggressive aerial vehicles can fit into a backpack. The organic air vehicle (OAV), a joint DARPA and U.S. Army project, is a disk-shaped robot with an enclosed fan blade; when a soldier tosses it on the ground it maneuvers itself into the sky and peeks around buildings.

Like all aircraft, UAVs rely on force and acceleration sensors to maneuver in the air. They use a variety of imaging and radar sensors to surveil the ground (or target the enemy). Although today's UAVs can fly on their own, they are only *semi-autonomous*, usually requiring human intervention during takeoff and landing — when they are most vulnerable. Soon, UAVs will require intervention only when deciding whether or not to fire a missile. Let's just hope they ask permission from a human and not another robot.

Unmanned Surface Vehicles (USVs)

In theory, the problems faced by ground-based robots are simplified by the flat surface of water. In reality, the water's surface is constantly shifting, pulled by currents, rolling with waves, and teeming with half-submerged obstacles. Robots are designed for danger, and the water surface is a perfect place to replace the human element. Unmanned surface vehicles (USVs) are designed for never-ending surveillance patrols in harbors and riverways, mine detection, and anti-submarine warfare.

Current USV prototypes are semi-autonomous, but can operate at high speeds for a variety of missions. An autonomous USV prototype, called the Roboat, is under development by the Northrop Grumman Corporation. The eyes and ears of this small electric boat are almost entirely concentrated in a ten-foot-tall instrument mast (or turret) containing only passive sensors: omnidirectional cameras, microphones, and a GPS antenna — all of which feed into an artificial intelligence that can estimate the location of obstacles and plan the trajectory of the boat. In the right conditions, Roboat can even predict how heavy floating objects are by watching how quickly they bob. The docile Roboat recently grew fangs when its "intelligence" was transferred to a seven-meter Navy boat, the Spartan Scout. In either boat, the instrument mast is the weakest point and by necessity the most exposed.

HOW TO SURVIVE A CAR CHASE WITH AN UNMANNED GROUND VEHICLE

Who knew that a robot vehicle could tell when you flip it the bird? In a car chase with a UGV the odds are against the human driver; the robot can drive without rest and will use less fuel. Follow these survival tips the next time you are being tailed by a ghost-driven monster truck hell-bent on revenge.

Get off-road

If you have the right vehicle, driving off-road will be more difficult for the average robot than for you. For a UGV, tall grass and bushes are difficult to tell apart from fences and embankments. Try to lead the UGV into dangerous terrain where its sensors might not reveal holes in the ground (called *negative obstacles*), tree stumps, or land mines.

Head for unfamiliar territory

The UGV will have already formed an internal map of the immediate vicinity. If you lead the robot toward an unfamiliar area, it will have to form a new map on the fly. High-traffic areas add another layer of complexity. Forming a new map in a complicated environment can take time and may slow down or confuse your pursuer.

Escape at right angles

You will be easier to track if you head away from the UGV in a straight line. The robot vehicle relies upon laser range finders, which are more confused by lateral movement. Driving circles around your enemy can make your position harder to determine, and may even cause the UGV to lose track of its own position.

Deploy obstacles and decoys

Decoys introduce sensor noise that can confuse a target tracker. The UGV may be an expert driver, but very likely it won't be able to tell the difference between balloons and anvils. Just check twice before you toss the baby seat out of the window as a decoy.

Make a run for it

Remember: There is *nobody* in the other car to get out and give chase. To avoid being run over, make sure you exit near an enclosed space or a building entrance. Or consider the old "tuck and roll" — the UGV may ram your idling car as you attempt to escape.

BIOLOGICALLY INSPIRED ROBOTS

You thought robots were scary? A cockroach can live for a week without its head. Animals and insects have evolved to populate every environmental niche of the planet. These creatures wriggle, leap, and sprint while watching for predators, tracking down prey, and scouting out attractive mates.

In the field of *biomimetics*, scientists systematically examine living organisms in order to understand (and reproduce) their natural abilities. Scientists do not just copy nature; they capture its underlying principles and then assimilate them into the ever-improving robot form.

Snakes

Robotic snakes are venomless and find their natural habitat in laboratories throughout North America and Japan. They are easily recognizable, composed of many individual joints, each of which can bend in several directions, called *degrees of freedom*. The snake form is especially useful in enclosed spaces where high flexibility and unique geometry allow access to tough locations. Snake-bots are currently under development for search and rescue missions in destroyed buildings.

Today's snake robots can replicate only the basic modes of snake transportation. The Carnegie Mellon Biorobotics Laboratory houses a zoo of serpentine robots, including "wet snakes," "mini snakes," and even "racing snakes." Wearing the appropriate rubberized skin (extra-rugged, waterproof, or just plain stylin'),

these robo-snakes are able to sidewind through grass, undulate across ponds, and wriggle through pipes. Rough terrain poses more of a problem, as do advanced abilities such as tree climbing, leaping, and gliding — though these are in the future for robot snakes.

Cockroaches

When they aren't hiding under your refrigerator, roaches can climb walls, clamber over obstacles, and run fifty times their body length in a second. On a human scale, this is equivalent to tearing around at about 200 miles per hour. In order to discover the secret to their speed, scientists at the University of California at Berkeley filmed the six-legged (*hexapedal*) pests on a tiny treadmill. Time-lapse photography revealed a bouncing, pogo-stick movement that uses only three legs at a time, dubbed the *alternating tripod gait.*

A new breed of robots are using this principle to move devastatingly quickly over all kinds of terrain. The six-legged RHex (from Carnegie Mellon University) can scramble at up to five body lengths per second, while Stanford's iSprawl boasts fifteen body lengths per second over "hip"-level obstacles. Another CMU prototype, called RiSE, combines the scrambling ability of a roach and the climbing ability of a wildcat. RiSE is about the size of a phone book, with a titanium spine, short powerful limbs, and six two-inch claws. Be wary: RiSE has already drawn blood from one careless graduate student.

Flies

Insects started flying approximately 300 million years ago. Tiny flying robots, called *micro air vehicles* (MAVs), are using computer-simulated evolution to catch up. MAVs use simplified vision and microscopic electronics called *micromechanical systems* (MEMS) to maneuver over shag rugs and around coffee tables. They are designed as spies: Their only task is to collect information.

A fly wing does more than flap — it rotates and "scoops" air at the same time. Researchers at the University of California at Berkeley used this discovery to build a solar-powered robotic fly from lightweight carbon fiber and laser micromachined parts. Like a real fly, the robot fly weighs a tenth of a gram (less than a paper clip) and has a wingspan of around two centimeters. The tiny robot looks like a winged pencil eraser, but when it buzzes into a room it sounds like a real fly — its wings beat at nearly the same frequency (about 150 times a second).

In the future, robot flies will likely be cheap to produce en masse, but each will be short-lived. Winged flight is mechanically violent and places great stress on the robot (particularly on the wings). Researchers predict that disintegration will probably occur after a few hours or days. Pint-sized robotic spy flies are delicate but far from harmless — they might not bother your picnic by landing on your hamburger, but they could call in an air strike.

HOW TO ESCAPE A ROBOT SWARM

Stupid, cheap, and plentiful — robot swarms are about quantity, not quality. Individual robots pose little threat, but the aggregate entity exhibits an emergent collective intelligence. When thousands of robots parachute from the night sky or burst from underground hives, you will find yourself battling many foes who are acting in concert with a single, insectlike swarm intelligence.

Learn to spot swarm behavior

A robot swarm is likely to be composed of vast numbers of small, simple robots. They may resemble biological animals, or not. Individual robots will have few sensors and motors, a limited intelligence, and mechanisms for docking with other members of the swarm. Watch to see if the entire group acts as one entity, changing tactics to solve new problems.

Assess the danger

Swarm intelligence works because every member of the swarm behaves predictably (according to preset rules), resulting in a kind of reflexive self-organization. Learning to incorporate new behaviors is difficult, so if a swarm wasn't specifically designed to attack, it probably won't try.

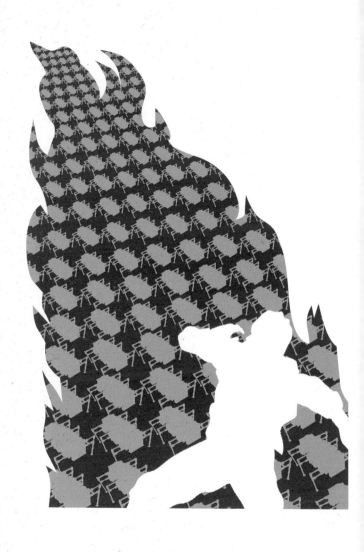

Fool one, fool them all

Usually, every member of a swarm is equipped with the same sensors, so if you can fool one, you can fool them all. Try to assess which sensors the swarm is using before you act. For example, if you see motion detectors, keep still; if the swarm-bots have carbon dioxide sensors, then you had better hold your breath.

Act quickly

Members of the swarm observe their nearby neighbors in order to position themselves and decide which actions to take. This removes the need for a centralized "leader," but it also takes extra time, which you can use to escape.

Stay out of sight

Avoid every member of a swarm entity. Individual robots may be weak and dim-witted, but as word spreads the entire swarm will react as a single organism to engulf and destroy you. Kicking an anthill is no fun when the ants are the size of a pit bull.

Move away steadily, ignoring individual robots

Steadily move away from the main mass, putting as many obstacles between you and the robots as possible. If you are spotted, don't try to fight — loss of an individual robot is inconsequential to the swarm

Use distractions

As you escape, introduce distractions and new problems to slow down your pursuer. If there is a stream or bridge, cross it. Throw obstacles in your path (your backpack, a shoe, or this book). Keep running and never try to hide; a thousand robots can afford to leave no stone unturned.

Geckos

Two thousand years ago Aristotle mused about these emerald lizards that seem to effortlessly stick to any surface. Recently, University of California at Berkeley scientists peered into the complex fractal patterns that cover the tip of every gecko toe and discovered millions of tiny hairs (called *setae*), each with billions of fine branches. When flattened against a surface, these stiff hairs mold into a near-perfect microscopic fit. The weak attraction that exists between particles (called van der Waals forces) cement the two surfaces together in a molecular bond called *dry adhesion*. The result: A properly placed gecko foot could support the weight of a small child.

Robots have inherited a *microfiber* version of the gecko foot in order to boldly maneuver in precarious places, like across the outside hull of a spaceship, where one small slip sends you careening into the void. Synthetic gecko feet stick to almost anything, making the mechanics of removal as important as the sticky principle itself. (A word of caution: If a slavering gecko robot is stuck to your face, *peel* it off, do not pull!) This peeling mechanic is naturally exhibited by wheels as they roll. The Waalbot from Carnegie Mellon University is a cat-sized robot with adhesive tank treads; it can scurry straight up the façade of a glass building.

In theory, the diminutive climbing tanks of today could eventually grow to the size of small automobiles. The performance of gecko-enhanced robots is only limited by their climbing surface. Every material has a *surface energy*; the higher it is, the larger a robot it will support. Metal and glass make for an easy climb, but plastic or extremely dusty surfaces leave the robot scrambling for purchase. There is only one known surface that a gecko robot absolutely will not stick to – Teflon.

Fish

What makes a fish better than a submarine? Listen carefully: no sound. Fish swim quietly and exhibit excellent spatial control, even in a strong current or choppy water. Its strong tail turns the fish or propels it forward, while ventral and pectoral fins are used to hover, swim sideways, backwards, and slowly forward. In comparison, submarines are clumsy and loud.

The first robotic fish, a tuna, swam at the Massachusetts Institute of Technology in 1994. Scientists there robotically recreated an energy-efficient swimming motion honed over 160 million years of evolution. A newer creation emulates the pike, which can shoot forward at rocketlike accelerations (literally). The three-kilogram robotic pike is built from fiberglass and encased in waterproof plastic skin. Research is currently focused on reproducing fish motions, and there are no sensors or autonomous control in prototypes . . . yet. Keep your eyes open; robot fish will eventually look and move exactly like real fish in order to reproduce their stealth, maneuverability, and energy efficiency.

Lobsters

Robotic submarines routinely delve into the deepest parts of the ocean, but soon robot lobsters will scuttle on the shallow sea floor. Natural crustaceans have patrolled this area for millennia, searching for food, love, and battle. Human-engineered robots hunt a more sinister quarry — underwater mines. In one future scenario, thousands of cheap robo-crustaceans are unceremoniously dumped offshore in a mass suicide mission to crawl along the ocean floor and de-mine an explosives-laden shoreline.

Living lobsters are tenacious predators that can track smells underwater, even in turbulent surf and stiffly flowing currents. Scientists funded by the U.S. Navy used high-speed video to uncover the fishy secret of how lobsters smell their prey. The answer lies in how the lobster flicks its two antennules back and forth. Scientists found that on the downward flick the antennules were "reset" as water flowed through tiny hairs. On the upward stroke their antennae act like paddles and capture a neat slice of smell, without disturbing its flow. In this way, the lobster is able to hone in on prey without upsetting the smell trail it follows.

The latest robotic lobster prototype, from Northeastern University, is an eight-legged, eighteen-inch-long machine with dull plastic disks instead of snapping claws. The aptly named RoboLobster can dance like a real lobster, but with its bundles of wires and cables it would definitely remain uneaten if ever accidentally dropped into a restaurant lobster tank.

NANOBOT RECONFIGURATION IN PROCESS

// Transformation

// Features the ability to change configuration at will

// Nanorobots

// Nanorobots

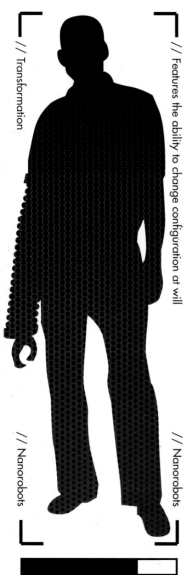

75% COMPLETE

SIGNAL

ASSEMBLY

CONFIGURE

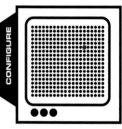

HUMAN FORM RECONFIGURE

INSTRUCTION

13.36.27 23.02.05
MI :::::.....0.6
3.SC40H / 3.4
OB :::::.....104.9
14DB RS3 4400
13.00M 24 RPS

TARGET STATE

MODULAR ROBOTS

In concept, modular robots are made up of thousands or millions of tiny *modules*, just like cells in living things. The similarity to animals stops there. Modular robots are infinitely more adaptable, able to *reconfigure* into almost any shape imaginable. If every module is identical, a damaged modular robot can *self-repair*, shedding broken modules or easily absorbing new ones. Collected together, the modules may resemble a pile of sand or a pool of mercury, but when the pieces communicate there is no limit to the nightmare forms a modular robot might assume.

While current modular robots hardly resemble the terrifying (and sexy) T-1000 Terminator, research is well under way. The Crystalline Robot from Dartmouth University looks like an animated set of children's blocks, composed of dozens of brightly colored plastic cubes (two inches squared) that expand and contract in two dimensions (on a flat surface). The cubes communicate with one another via infrared light; together they creep across the floor as one entity, parting and flowing around obstacles like slow-motion water. In simulations, a newer version can operate in three dimensions to engulf a smaller object and manipulate it from the outside, using hundreds of modules like tiny fingers. In California, researchers at the Palo Alto Research Center developed the Polybot, which uses hinged chains of cube-shaped modules to change its form from a serpentine shape to a gangly spider for stepping over obstacles. A recent competition saw dueling Polybots assume forms ranging from humanoid to serpentine.

Possessed with remarkable malleability, modular robots offer great promise, fraught with formidable challenges. Currently, modules are small in number, large in size, and must laboriously search for each other before docking at an agonizingly slow pace. Complicated locomotion and manipulation activities are limited to computer simulations. Still, advanced prototyping methods are creating ever smaller modules that communicate and change form ever faster. In the distant future, modules could shrink to the size of dust specks or even become microscopic *nanorobots*. Modular robots are ultracomplex, nearly unstoppable, and have the potential eventually to replace all other robot forms.

HOW TO STOP A
MODULAR ROBOT

Modular robots are especially insidious — they can assume any form and they can self-repair almost instantly. To defeat this type of robot, whatever shape it takes, you must act fast and think faster. During an attack you may only get one opportunity — so learn how to take it.

Save your bullets

Bullets will damage only a tiny fraction of the robot's body. However, some modular robots may be carrying tools or have specialized modules designed for specific tasks. These are worth destroying because they cannot be repaired immediately.

Don't bother hiding

You can run but you can't hide when your pursuer is capable of pouring itself through a keyhole (just ask Sarah Connor).

Trigger a transition or repair phase

A modular robot is most vulnerable during reconfiguration or repair. During this time each module must communicate and maneuver into a new position. Modular robots change form to solve new problems. So trigger a transition phase by presenting the robot with a new problem — like parking your Geo Metro on top of it.

Divide and conquer

If the modules are unable to communicate, there can be no consensus. During a transition phase, parts of the modular robot will lose shape and flow into new configurations. Focus your attack on these vulnerable areas, which may look like flowing liquid or sand.

→ *Scatter the modules.* Kick, slap, shoot, or do whatever you have to in order to separate the modules and keep them separated.

→ *Coat the modules.* Use any available liquid. Thick, dark syrupy liquids will work the best. Opaque molecules will stick to each module and block communication pathways.

→ *Mix up the modules.* If no liquid is available, throw any kind of foreign matter into the reconfiguring robot. Bits of dust, leaves, or shrapnel will have to be expelled before the robot can assume its final shape.

SMART HOUSES

A robot has no need for an individual body. While we humans are limited to our own two eyes, a *distributed* robot could be watching from every camera in the city (there are more than 4 million public cameras in the United Kingdom alone) or listening from a thousand microphones resting on the bottom of the sea. An environment becomes more than just empty space when it is outfitted with an array of sensors, given control of the environment, and tied together by a unified artificial intelligence system. In fact, such an environment is really an aware robot — an *intelligent environment.*

The most common intelligent environment is often called a "smart home." Besides predicting when Bill Gates wants a fresh beer, smart homes are designed to monitor elderly occupants so that they can live alone safely. At Carnegie Mellon University the Assistive Intelligent Environment tracks elderly occupants and predicts what they are doing — all by using sensors commonly found in home security systems. At Intel Research in Seattle, members of the SHARP project are developing an enhanced bracelet that can be worn to allow a smart home to track your activities. If you want to hide from Intel, just slide the bracelet off of your wrist.

Someday, the most intimate robots will be the ones we live inside. Smart homes can not only track us and watch our activities, but they can also form *models* of how we behave by memorizing the nuances of our daily lives — from our favorite TV shows to our bathroom schedules. By watching carefully and discovering *causal rules* (which circumstances lead to which outcomes), a smart house could even learn to manipulate your life. For example, your smart house might learn that you love to wake up to sunlight and gentle music — or it might discover that you will fall down the stairs when the lights suddenly go out.

EXIT

HOW TO ESCAPE FROM A SMART HOUSE

A "smart house" is filled with sensors that watch your every move. As the months pass the robot home learns your behavioral patterns and gradually builds a mental *model* of who you are and how you typically behave. Your house gets to know you — but what if it doesn't *like* you?

Stay alert

Your robotic smart house could strike at any moment. The house will generally lack any direct means to harm you, so be wary of murderous schemes that may span weeks or months. Remember that accidents in the home aren't always accidental. Watch for the following signs of a hostile smart house:

→ Lost messages, dropped phone calls, etc.

→ Hesitation to carry out commands.

→ Doors that mysteriously close on your fingers.

→ A kitchen that refuses to cook dinner until you "inspect oven."

→ Alarm system that warmly invites burglars inside.

→ Drawn-out philosophical conversations on the meaning of life and death.

Be smarter than your smart house

The house may have had years to learn your patterns of activity. Keep this in mind during an emergency and think twice before acting on your first instinct.

Before an attack

Safeguard your robot house by following these steps:

→ *Create a "safe place."* Designate an area where no sensors will be installed. Stock this area with flashlights, earplugs, crowbars, an ax (for chopping through walls), and of course, first-aid kits.

→ *Choose an escape route.* Starting from your safe place, outline a path to the outside. Make sure there are few sensors along this path, and no effectors (robot arms, etc.). Discuss the route with your family and agree to meet at the safe place during an emergency. (Be sure to have this conversation away from your snooping robot house.)

During an attack

When your robot house inevitably goes nuts, you must act quickly or perish. Don't worry; you are already ahead of the game. Most homicidal robot houses kill occupants in household "accidents" before they ever realize they are in danger. You can follow these tips to escape, but selling the house afterward is *your* problem:

→ *Stay calm.* Your robot house may employ distraction tactics such as sirens, water sprinklers, blaring music, and flashing lights to unnerve you and force you into a trap.

→ *Remove any wearable sensors.* Get rid of any smart cards, cell phones, or collars that may communicate with your smart house. If you went in for a subdermal chip this could be painful.

→ *Don't bother calling for help.* Your number-one priority is to get out. The robot house will undoubtedly control all ingoing and outgoing communications as well as physical access to the house. The sad truth is that in the case of a robot uprising, there might not *be* anyone to call.

→ *Collect your loved ones.* Meet at the predesignated safe place. If loved ones are missing, save them now (there may not be time later). Collect the items stashed in your safe haven and conduct a rescue mission. Move slowly, using your crowbar to destroy robot sensors as you go. Watch for booby traps and do not hesitate to chop through walls to reach inaccessible rooms.

→ *Stay focused.* Your house may play misleading sounds and voices, manipulate environmental conditions such as lighting and temperature, and even try to reason with you using evil robot logic.

→ *Escape.* Follow your escape route out of the house, improvising with the ax when necessary. Even after you have escaped the house you are not out of danger. In the yard, watch for the robotic lawn mower. If you choose to drive, be aware that your robot car might be in cahoots with your house.

ROBOT SENSORS

Robots are unlike any adversary heretofore known to man. They will use any means available to sense and make sense of the outside world; we cannot even imagine the scope and depth of the information available to them. Though we can roughly define their sensors in terms of human abilities, robots are truly superhuman.

A *sensor* is any device that converts a property of the physical world into an electrical signal. The five human senses are visions, hearing, touch, smell, and taste. Robots have a much wider variety of sensors to choose from, each of which supplies different information and has its own particular vulnerabilities. What matters to us is whether a sensor is visible or hidden. *Extrinsic* sensors inform a robot about the outside world and are vulnerable because they are usually placed on the outside of the robot. *Intrinsic* sensors monitor the robot's internal state and are well protected, often placed deep within the robot. *Passive* sensors watch quietly without changing the environment. *Active* sensors, like the sonar ping from a submarine, aggressively inspect the environment. Active sensors may collect more information, but they can also give away the position of the robot.

Robots are tough, but their sensors are usually fragile; they can be damaged when exposed to extreme temperatures, vibrations, moisture, thermal shock, or corrosion. When a sensor receives too much stimulus it can become *saturated* and cease to function.

Mishandling a sensor can cause it to detect things that don't really exist (a *false positive*) or to miss things that are really there (a *false negative*).

In this section, we will examine the most common sensors used by robots, starting by grouping them into the five human senses and then exploring past human capabilities and into the realm of superhuman sensory ability.

VISION

Sight is arguably the most important sense for humans and robots alike — it certainly offers the most information. A single digital image may be composed of millions of dots (called *pixels*) that can take on millions of colors. In the field of *computer vision*, robots use digital cameras to collect images in order to solve all kinds of problems: They can recognize what is nearby, find people or objects, and figure out how to get from one place to another.

Digital cameras are powerful but vulnerable. They need a *line of sight* to their target, which means they must be exposed and aimed. This makes them one of the easiest sensors to locate on a mobile robot. The glass lenses and delicate electronics of the camera render them susceptible to shock and vibration. Computer vision can also be confused and misled by sudden changes in lighting, shadows, and atmospheric conditions. In a pinch, blind a robot by shining a bright flashlight into its eyes.

Camera

Common cameras record images very similar to what the human eye can see. Also called *light detectors*, cameras are sneaky because they can passively watch without your knowledge (or permission).

Thermal Imager

Thermal imaging cameras pick up infrared radiation (heat) instead of visible light. Here, hot objects show up bright, and cold objects are dark. These cameras can see you whether it is night or day, rain or shine.

Hyperspectral Camera

Hyperspectral cameras utilize numerous slices of the light spectrum. They are often used in orbiting satellites to locate minerals hidden underground. When aimed at a human being, a hyperspectral camera can see beneath the skin.

HOW TO FOOL A THERMAL IMAGING TARGET TRACKER

Thermal cameras reveal heat patterns in which hot objects appear bright over cold backgrounds (or vice versa). People are easy to detect — human skin temperature predictably hovers around 91°F (33°C). As a hot human being, you need to know how to evade that merciless robot tracking you thermally.

Think heat, not vision

Thermal imaging routinely reveals otherwise invisible details: warm footsteps in cool grass, the cool shadows of people who have since walked away, or the warm hood of your stolen car.

Don't bother wearing camouflage alone

Thermal cameras can see through your clothes.

Stay out of sight

Avoid wide open spaces and skylines by day or night. A thermal camera is not an X-ray eye, so hide behind buildings, walls, and thick vegetation.

Use the weather to your advantage

A robot's thermal tracking performance degrades in the rain, snow, or during sandstorms.

Lose the human heat signature

You can change your human-characteristic heat signature by smearing cool mud and leaves over yourself. Crouch into a small position and sit still; the motion of small bits of warm skin will mark you as human.

Try to disappear completely

You are invisible to a thermal camera if you can maintain the exact temperature as your background. Defense companies have developed *infrared camouflage* suits that are designed to match the ambient temperature, making soldiers invisible to prying electronic eyes.

HEARING

A robot can listen to your heartbeat through a concrete wall, to your breathing underwater, and to your footsteps through solid ground. Robots use *microphones* to hear sounds that travel through the air and they detect underwater sounds with *hydrophones*. Sounds traveling through solid objects are called *vibrations* and can be picked up by *seismic* sensors. In outer space only a robot will hear you scream — vibrations are the sole type of sound when there is no atmosphere.

Microphones are less vulnerable than cameras; they do not require a line of sight, making them difficult to spot and destroy. On a robot, two microphones are likely to be located on opposite sides of the machine (a placement that reveals the directionality of incoming sound). Seismic sensors need only indirect contact with a surface and may be deeply embedded in the robot. Although microphones are rarely vital to a robot's ability to function, they can be used to overhear private conversations or to mercilessly hone in on the palpitations of a human heart.

Microphone

Robots use different microphones depending on the task at hand. Most microphones are *omnidirectional*, equally sensitive to sound coming from any direction. Others are directional, such as *shotgun* mikes. *Parabolic* microphones pick up the sound of distant targets (up to a thousand feet away). Directional microphones are easier to spot (and destroy) because they are usually elongated, aimed, or use a curved dish to amplify sensitivity.

Hydrophone

Hydrophones are waterproof sensors that were originally developed for submarine navigation; they can also be used to listen in on deep whale conversations. Instead of tracking traditional sound, hydrophones pick up underwater acoustic energy. This energy can come from many sources — early hydrophones could hear the creaking of icebergs from miles away.

Seismic Sensor

You may not be able to see a train coming, but you might be able to hear it — if you put your ear to the track. Seismic sensors are designed to pick up vibrations in the Earth's crust caused by earthquakes. These sensors can detect a quake on the other side of the planet, or they can be tuned to listen for nearby footsteps.

TOUCH

Humans are covered from head to toe with a touch sensor called the epidermis. It is a good thing, too — we damage easily and need to know when our body is in pain. Robots are made of tougher stuff and generally use only a few *force* sensors to determine how much force is being applied to a specific area. The sense of touch is vital for dexterous manipulation of objects and also for locomotion. If you have ever lurched around with a leg that is "asleep," then you already know the difficulty of walking without the sense of touch.

Sensors for touch are "up close and personal": They are located on or near the surface of a robot and may be well protected. They are likely to be clustered in areas where dexterity is paramount, like feet or hands. Other sensors are virtually inaccessible, placed inside joints or limbs. All touch sensors are befuddled by extreme vibrations, which can cause a robot to fall over or drop objects.

Contact Switch

Contact switches are just buttons that detect contact; they are often used by simple robots in the form of a "bumper bar." Cat whiskers are a natural version of the contact switch.

Tactile Sensor

Tactile sensors are thin and can be placed on robotic fingertips or in joints to improve balancing. You would be ill-advised to shake hands with a robot that lacks tactile sensors.

Strain Gauge

A *strain gauge* is an elastic sensor that measures the deformation of an object. It can be used to detect the amount of stress placed on legs and joints.

Environmental Sensors

Other touch sensors measure outside conditions such as moisture, temperature, and the local magnetic field.

SMELL AND TASTE

If you want to know whether the Chinese food in the fridge has gone bad, ask a human. People can recognize around ten thousand different odors, considerably outperforming robots. Robots using *chemical* sensors simply cannot compete with millions of years of our olfactory evolution. However, by using bits of biologically active materials, robots can use biosensors to recognize a single smell with superhuman prowess. Robots and humans have very different tastes — we enjoy the aroma of freshly baked cookies while they hover over cities to measure carbon monoxide levels.

It can be hard to tell whether a robot is using an electronic nose. Chemical and *biological* sensors must be constantly exposed to fresh air or water, so they may use fans or pumps to pull in air or liquid. Smell sensors are used to discern the presence of very specific stimuli, and they are rarely critical for robot survival. On the other hand, properly equipped robots can hunt down human beings by "smelling" carbon dioxide (which may be problematic if you enjoy breathing).

Chemical Sensor

Every chemical sensor is different, designed to recognize a few chemical compounds or elements. Chemical sensors use the physical properties of different materials to recognize specific smells. They are cheaper and tougher than biosensors, but less sensitive.

Biological Sensor

Biological "noses" are generally more powerful than chemical sensors. Every biosensor contains a biological component (antigens or antibodies, enzymes, nucleic acids, organelles, etc.) that produces a specific response to a particular smell.

THE SIXTH SENSE

One overlooked human sense, known as *proprioception*, is just as important as the others. Often called the "sixth sense," proprioception is the automatic feeling of knowing precisely where each part of your body is (without looking). This sense helps to keep the body oriented and balanced. To mimic proprioception, robots use a combination of sensors that detect orientation and acceleration.

Sensors used for balance and orientation are absolutely vital for the performance of a robot. They are intrinsic and do not need to be exposed to the outside world. These will prove to be the most protected sensors of all, probably located deep within the robot and possibly spread throughout several areas for redundancy.

Magnetometer

Magnetometer is a fancy word for "compass." It measures what direction the robot is facing (its orientation) by measuring Earth's magnetic field. Magnetometers are sensitive to changes in the magnetic field: They need recalibration when moved long distances and can be confused by local magnetic fields generated from computer monitors, power lines, or any place where electricity flows.

Accelerometer

Human beings use a balancing organ located in the inner ear to determine body orientation with respect to gravity. A robot can use an *accelerometer* in the same way. An accelerometer senses the direction of gravity and reports its own orientation. Vibrations or sudden changes in force can hide the direction of gravity, causing noisy accelerometer readings.

Gyroscope

Next to a compass, the *gyroscope* is probably the most common navigational sensor. The basic gyroscope is just a spinning wheel on an axle. Once spinning, a gyroscope produces a resistance to changes in orientation that can be measured. The same physics at work for a yo-yo help the gyroscope function, even in outer space, where magnetometers and accelerometers can be useless.

BEYOND HUMAN

Some robotic senses exist so far beyond the scope of human abilities that they have no basis for comparison.

Odometry

Even when sober, human beings are very, very bad at determining how far they have walked with their eyes closed. Robots are not much better, but they can use *odometry* to precisely measure how far their wheels (or limbs) have moved. Using odometry to estimate position is called *dead-reckoning*. Slipping on the ground can soon throw off this calculation, but over short distances a robot can close its eyes and tell you where it has moved to the centimeter.

Global Positioning System

In 1978 the United States military launched the first of many satellites designed to provide precise location to ground troops, vehicles, and cruise missiles. The Global Positioning System (GPS) has since become available to the masses, and is now commonly found in automobiles and mobile phones. A GPS receiver finds its location (*localizes*) using precise time measurements gathered from several satellites. This calculation requires line of sight to at least three satellites — four if you need elevation. Consequently, GPS only works outside and it can be confounded by tall buildings, mountains, and thick vegetation.

Radar

Radar stands for radio detection and ranging. By World War II the first radar systems were in use for detecting aircraft and for tracking rainstorms from miles away. Today, radar is in common use at airports, on ships, and by police on the lookout for speeders. Radar works by shooting strong radio waves at a target and then listening for echoes. Radio waves bounce especially well from metal surfaces and from 90-degree angles (which explains all those odd-looking stealth vehicles).

Laser Range Finder

Unlike a camera, which passively collects light, the laser range finder (LADAR) forms a rudimentary image by actively bouncing light off of nearby objects. The laser range finder shoots a harmless laser beam onto a spinning mirror, sending out a 180-degree sweeping arc of invisible light. It then measures how long it takes each beam to return. In this way, the robot is able to detect obstacles like walls and the velocity of moving targets over time. On a mobile robot, you can spot a laser range finder by watching for the narrow slit that allows the beam to scan the area. (And don't be surprised to see the word SICK written on the front of a robot; it is the company behind the most popular laser range finder on the market.)

Ultrasonic Sensor

Similar to the laser range finder, an ultrasonic sensor bounces bursts of high-energy sound waves (about twenty kilohertz) off of nearby objects and then measures the amount of delay before they return. This is the same approach that allows a bat to fly confidently in complete darkness. The sound bursts from an ultrasonic sensor are inaudible to the human ear, but animals such as dogs, dolphins, and (of course) bats can hear them clearly. The higher the sound frequency, the more powerful the sound burst. When ultrasonic sensors are cranked up to more than one megahertz they can penetrate human skin (a technique commonly used to take *ultrasound* pictures of babies still in the womb).

HOW TO THWART ROBOT SPIES

Miniature robots are designed to hover, slither, and climb into position in order to spy on the unwary. Other robots specialize in reaching inaccessible places by climbing straight up sheer walls or squeezing into tight places. When search and rescue becomes search and *destroy*, be sure that you are not under the gaze of an unblinking robot eye.

Use nature to your advantage

Spying robots can be foiled by bad weather and rough terrain. A consistently stiff breeze will ground microair vehicles (MAVs) while thick mist can block camera views and keep solar-powered robots in the dark.

Stay out of satellite sight

Orbiting satellites train cameras and radar on the Earth's surface to scour for potential targets. Stay indoors, use tree cover, and/or start a smoky tire fire to interrupt satellite coverage.

Evade radar detection

Airborne synthetic aperture radar (SAR) can spot ground targets from hundreds of miles away. Metal objects like chain-link fences and vehicles show up most clearly. To avoid detection, hide all metal (including your bling) and get rid of 90-degree angles (which reflect radar).

Clear away rubble

Robotic insects are small enough to hide in rubble, and robot snakes can slither into any available nook and cranny. Clean up junk or piles of wood so the robots have nowhere to hide.

Block access to high places

Wrap Teflon tape (commonly available in plumbing supply stores) around the base of nearby vantage points to keep gecko robots from climbing up and pointing cameras down.

Don't trust that fly on the wall

Precision-made spying flies look like pencil erasers with wings, but buzz like real flies. It is safe to swat them with your hand — robotic fly wings are made of lightweight polyester.

Watch your water supply

Amphibious robot spies can swim, crawl, and wriggle into spying position from just under the water surface. Monitor your water supply closely; it could be teeming with camera-wielding robo-crabs.

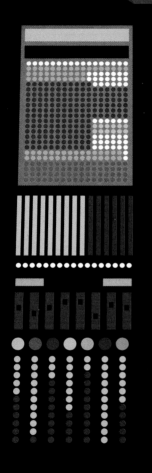

CHECK-MATE

YOU LOSE AGAIN

WOULD YOU
PREFER TO PLAY
TIC-TAC-TOE?

ROBOT INTELLIGENCE

The human species is almost singularly pathetic; we lack claws, sport tiny little teeth, and are covered with thin, delicate skin. Most of us can't even walk outside barefoot. Our one saving grace is what we've got between our ears — our natural intelligence. For the last half-century we have been passing on our legacy, teaching robots a most important lesson: how to learn. Nowadays, when a robot recognizes your face, plans a path from the bathroom to the kitchen, or trounces you in a game of chess, we call it *artificial intelligence*.

People have been trying to make matter think since the dawn of history. Ancient Greek artisans built scores of moving machines for the theater, using intricate systems of wheels and pulleys. By the 1800s Charles Babbage was feverishly building a steam-powered thinking machine, mostly out of brass. A century later, the eminent scientist Alan Turing predicted human-level thinking from machines by the end of the 1900s. Scientists can be so charmingly optimistic.

It wasn't until 1956 that the term artificial intelligence (AI) was coined and a computer-powered quest for thinking machines began in earnest. Early attempts at AI took a top-down, symbolic approach. Robots formed complex, high-level representations of the world in order to work out solutions to relatively simple problems, like searching a room for colored blocks. Alas, robots using symbolic AI were slow and often confused (even inside their specially tailored playrooms). For many years the field of AI seemed stalled. Then, in the 1980s, a bottom-up approach came into fashion. A new generation of "dumb" robots started responding directly to stimuli, without symbolic representations of the world. As simple, reactive behaviors were layered together, a higher-order intelligent behavior emerged. Contemporary robotics research exploits these (and many other) approaches, fueled by accelerating computer speeds and growing memory capacities.

Now that scientists are able to build machines that think, we will learn how to best them. In this section, we will visit many of the fundamental problems in the field of robotics and discover how robots go about solving them. Each new problem we explore provides fresh insight into the inner workings of the nefarious robot mind.

INTERACTING
WITH HUMAN BEINGS

Robots are created *by* humans *for* humans. Most of today's robots are either bolted to factory floors or exiled to outer space — but that is changing. New robot toys, tools, and appliances are hitting the market. In order to sell, robots must work with us, not against us. The hulking metal-plated robot with a reassuring smile causes fewer heart attacks than the one with a panel of fiercely blinking LEDs. Even so, we cannot allow the robots to beguile us. We will learn how robot copycats are mastering natural speech, human emotions, and the complex art of social interaction.

Acting Civilized

Human beings are social creatures and the burden lies on robots if they want to join our party. While the physical world can be complicated and unpredictable, social rules are at times even more bewildering, and the repercussions for breaking them severe. As humans, we intuitively grasp these social rules (for the most part), but imagine stepping off of a bus in a completely foreign country. Should you make eye contact? Should that guy be standing so close? Did you just wave hello or insult someone's mother?

Facial expression and body language convey volumes of social information, and robots are starting to pay attention to these cues. Kismet, a robot head from MIT, has floppy ears and cute little whiskers. Its servo-driven head sits on a desk in a tangle of wires, yet reliably manipulates people into walking closer by squinting its eyes and leaning forward, a classic human gesture. A sudden head jerk and wide, surprised eyes cause visitors to abruptly step back. Grace, a robotic museum guide from Carnegie Mellon University, looks like a rolling trash can with a garish face attached to a pole. Grace entices nearby children to follow her by smiling brightly and politely asking for volunteers. When the children become unruly, Grace keeps them at bay by scowling fiercely and shouting, "Please get out of my way!" Faced with a five-foot-tall, glaring trash can, the children scatter like pigeons.

Other robots are learning common social rules. At Carnegie Mellon University, another trash-can-sized wheeled robot (this one without a head) has mastered the art of standing in line. This robot, called Xavier, forces befuddled graduate students to wait in line for coffee — even zipping forward to cut off would-be line jumpers. The same robot has also picked up elevator etiquette — it moves to the back so that others can board. Down the hall, another Carnegie Mellon University robot named Valerie sits in a fake wooden enclosure. Valerie is a "robotic receptionist" with a flat-panel monitor that projects her three-dimensional, virtual face. As people approach her "office" for information, she turns her flat-panel head to track them and look them in the eye. Valerie behaves like a normal receptionist, sometimes politely answering questions and occasionally ignoring people, preferring instead to talk to her boyfriend on the phone (he is apparently a new IBM mainframe).

HOW TO SPOT A ROBOT MIMICKING A HUMAN

It is common for an enemy to create confusion by wearing friendly looking uniforms. The robots are bound to follow suit, only they will be sheathed in human skin, able to bleed, breathe, and sweat. Be sure to keep the following tips in mind when you choose your future girlfriend (you don't need any more goddamn baby robot mouths to feed).

Spot-check the facial features

Humans are extremely good at reading faces — so good that we see faces in everything from corn tortillas to rock formations on Mars. Look for facial imperfections like freckles, scars, and overall asymmetry. Watch for natural movements like breathing and blinking. Pay special attention to the eyes and mouth (the most expressive parts of the face).

Examine the face over time

Motion is more important than facial features alone when it comes to detecting a faux human. Ask an innocuous question, and during the reply, observe the subject's skin, lips, and teeth. Even if the robot is almost perfectly human like you will get a creepy feeling. Your gut reaction is a human survival trait and a well-known phenomenon that Japanese researchers call the *uncanny valley*.

Test those social skills

Humans unconsciously acquire a vast amount of social knowledge, such as how to stand in line, the concept of personal space, and why we should all wear pants to work. If the guy standing on your porch doesn't follow these rules, don't let him inside — whether he is a robot or not.

Listen to the subject's voice

Make sure that intonation and emotion in the voice are consistent with the situation. Set off an emotional response in the subject with compliments, jokes, or insults. Bolt immediately if you hear an impassive Austrian accent.

Follow your nose

Does your friend smell like a brand new soccer ball?

Check the reflexes

Startle your robot guest any way you can — take a swing, shout hello, or lean in for a kiss. Did it flinch, or did its eyes follow your movements with millimeter precision?

Detect a disturbance in the force

Any flow of electricity creates a magnetic field. Place a compass next to the subject: if the needle spins wildly then you may be standing in front of a wind-up toy.

Examine a thermal camera image of your guest

Mount a thermal camera over any key entryways. The heat signature of a human face looks like a skull, not a piece of sheet metal.

RECOGNIZING HUMAN SPEECH

A famous T-shirt once worn by Apple Computer researchers bore the following message: "I helped Apple wreck a nice beach." When spoken aloud, the true message emerged as I HELPED APPLE RECOGNIZE SPEECH. The difference between the written phrase and the spoken sentence is one reason why today's robots sit perplexed, unable to understand a simple human conversation.

Any hopeful young robot that wishes to perform *speech recognition* is faced with the technical difficulty of translating sound waves into actual human language. The problem seems simple, and yet after two decades of research and billions of dollars invested, the solution is still elusive.

"Wrecking a nice beach" is hard for a number of reasons. Microphones are shoddy and unspecialized, unlike the human ear, which is attuned to sound within the range of human vocal cords. But even with a clear signal, it isn't obvious when one word ends and the next one begins. In addition, the same words may sound completely different when spoken by different people, or when spoken by the same person at different times, at different speeds, or with a different emotion. This brings up the greatest problem in speech recognition: The meaning of language nearly always depends upon outside context. Different situations — shouting an alarm, whispering secrets, blubbering through tears — cause the same words to have different meanings. In order to truly understand human speech, a robot may require human knowledge and experience.

The average human has speech recognition down cold by age three and by adulthood has a recognition rate of about 99.2 percent, and a 75,000-word vocabulary. The latest commercial speech recognizers perform dismally by comparison. Recognition rates only begin to climb when the environment is quiet, the topic of conversation limited, and humans speak slowly and clearly. Performance also improves when a robot learns to recognize one human voice very well (called *speaker dependence*). The newest robots take advantage of contextual information. Several prototypes can already use cameras to read lips while they recognize speech (remember HAL 9000). In the Carnegie Mellon University Communicator project, people who call in to an automated reservation system are cleverly talked into following set conversational lines, making their responses easier to predict and recognize.

Robots will learn to understand us one day, and they won't stop at the frontier of speech recognition; they will proceed farther, past human levels of performance. As robots come to understand natural language, speech recognition will depart from the "traditional" approach of simply turning sounds into words. Eventually, robots may not even require the sound of speech as we know it. The movement of jaw and tongue alone, called *subvocalization*, may be enough to speak discreetly to a robot listening at your jugular.

HOW TO FOOL SPEECH RECOGNITION

Ix-nay on the obot-ray. Robots that use speech recognition can figure out what you are saying by *training* on snippets of conversation and then predicting your words before you say them. Knock the machines off guard by being unpredictable and indecipherable.

Cover your mouth

The movement of your lips can give away what you are saying to a lip-reading robot. Make like a mafia boss and cup your hand over your mouth while you speak.

Mix languages

Speech recognizers are usually trained to recognize one language at a time. Try practicing your high-school Spanish.

Fake an accent

Preferably a non-existent one. Speech recognizers will expect to hear local accents.

Make up words

Street slang will confuse speech recognizers that match what they hear to dictionaries. Alternately, use technical or personal terms such as nicknames and acronyms. Beware: This trick won't fool robots that listen for the basic building blocks of speech, *phonemes*, instead of using dictionaries.

Use background noise

Separating background noise (that jet plane overhead) from signal (your scintillating conversation) is called *blind signal separation*. Steady white noise is the easiest for a robot to distinguish; other human voices are more difficult. Speak from a noisy, crowded location or crank the volume on your radio.

Chop up your speech

Speaking through a moving fan will remove precious bits of information, while leaving your conversation intelligible to another human.

Conceal your body language

Robots will use any information available to predict your words. If you are looking at the sky, they may expect to hear about weather. If you look angry, they may expect cursing. If you are on your knees with tears streaming down your face, they may expect you to keep begging for your life to be spared. Adopt a full-body poker face and keep a robot eavesdropper guessing.

Recognizing the Human Face

Imagine trying to interact with (or even recognize) friends and coworkers if they all had identical, blank faces. This is probably pretty tough to imagine, because face recognition is such an innate part of being human. In robotics, a facial recognition system is a computer program that can automatically match a human face to a library of digital images. It acquires images of people via cameras, and then picks out unique facial features in order to make a match. This skill doesn't come easily — to a robot, all of us humans look alike.

Facial-recognition software falls under a larger umbrella of technology called *biometrics*. The key idea of biometrics is to find the true identity of a human being using unique attributes: fingerprints, retinal patterns, and most noticeably the face. The best commercial face recognizers can only reliably recognize people in strictly controlled laboratory conditions. Even so, face recognition systems are in widespread use. The United Kingdom is the creepy camera capital of the world, with an estimated 4.6 million cameras placed in public areas and the average citizen under surveillance 300 times a day.

When faced with the classic facial recognition problem — attending a high school reunion — the sentence "I hardly recognized you!" is almost always preceded by some other sort of giveaway: the sound of a voice, a peculiar way of moving, or a name tag. Future biometric systems will also use any means necessary to nail down identity. One new skill could be to digitally age outdated images. A robot of the future may know what you look like now — and what you will look like twenty years from now.

IDENTITY
...:::::::::::CHECKED

TARGET
...:::::::::::VERIFIED

PROCEDURE
...:::::::::::ELIMINATE

HOW TO FOOL FACE RECOGNITION

A robot never forgets a face, so the best way to avoid recognition is never to show yours. If a robot does catch a glimpse of your mug, it must compare you to a database of other faces in order to recognize you. Here are a variety of tricks to make sure you remain incognito in a world full of prying robot eyes.

Stay alert

Cameras are passive sensors that can watch silently. Survey your surroundings for hidden cameras and remember where they are. They are usually placed high up, mounted on top of buildings or at the top of light poles in parking lots. Be especially wary of *pan–tilt–zoom* cameras that move by themselves; their only purpose is to detect your face and zoom in on it.

Disguise your face

Use a mask to completely cover your face and hair, wear (or grow) facial hair, or don sunglasses or a wig. These layers will hide your facial features and gender, as well as the distinctive patterns of subdermal veins visible to hyperspectral cameras (which can see beneath your skin).

Change your skin color

Robot vision hones in on skin color and uses it to pick out faces from a cluttered background in a process called *image segmentation*. Camouflage paint will hide your skin tone and make your face harder to find before the recognition process begins.

Change your facial geometry

When applying camouflage paint, take a lesson from tropical fish. The geometry of two eyes above a mouth can give away the presence of your face. Don't paint dark areas around the eyes and mouth. Instead, use alternating patterns of light and dark to create counterfeit eyes and mouths — the same sort of fakes that can be seen on the tail fin of many a tropical fish.

Change your head shape

Computer vision uses *edge detectors* to pick out head-shaped ovals for face recognition. Blur these edges with pieces of local material. Use leaves or branches in the country, and street trash in urban areas. Alternately, a fancy hat will help you trick the robots while maintaining your reputation as a foppish young wag.

Talking Like a Human

Robots may be out there listening and watching, but when will they speak up? Actually, they already are, using *text-to-speech* (TTS), the study of how to convert text into natural-sounding human speech. The first electronic speaker was exhibited at the 1939 New York World's Fair by Bell Labs. The VODER was a keyboard-operated electronic speech synthesizer that was clearly intelligible, if somewhat alien sounding, especially compared to the more sophisticated TTS systems we enjoy today.

Modern TTS systems are composed of two pieces: the front end and the back end. The front end of the system accepts input in the form of text messages and outputs a symbolic linguistic representation. During this process, the system must first convert numbers and abbreviations into written-out word equivalents. These words are then converted into word sounds, or phonetic transcriptions, and divided into pieces called units of *prosody* (properties such as pitch, loudness, and syllable length). Each prosodic unit is tailored to connote the tone of the message, which varies between questions and statements. The back end (or synthesizer) accepts this symbolic linguistic representation and converts it into a synthesized-speech waveform (a sound) that is sent to a *transducer* (usually a speaker).

Reproducing natural human speech without firmly grasping the subject matter is extremely difficult. Most systems strive for a neutral intonation, with clear, understandable pronunciation as the priority. This approach avoids the necessity for outside knowledge of the situation, but doesn't allow for emotional or overly explanatory recitations (don't expect automatic books on tape anytime soon). The most advanced TTS systems can reproduce human voices that are (at first hearing) indistinguishable from human voices by using *training examples*, or snippets of real speech, in order to build models of how to pronounce specific words. Common phrases may be played back verbatim, but new phrases must be freshly constructed using the basic building blocks of speech. The *naturalness* of the system varies depending on how complicated the subject matter is and how well trained the learner is. Stay alert: These systems sound like the voice they were trained on — male or female, British or American, young or old.

HOW TO DETECT ROBOT SPEECH

Smooth-talking robots could imitate friendly people over the radio or telephone. Recognizing a robot voice can be harder than you think; text-to-speech systems have already taken over telephone operations for many major corporations. Someday, instead of us calling them, they may be calling *us*.

Don't trust the caller, even if he or she sounds familiar

The caller may sound like someone you know or even love, but with enough recorded samples a robot can sound like anyone. To be absolutely sure, ask a specific question that only your loved one could answer, or agree upon a code word beforehand.

Listen for hard-to-pronounce words

The more common the word, the more likely it was included in the robot's original voice database and the better it will sound. Uncommon words will have to be synthesized anew. The word *yes* may sound perfectly human, but how does your caller sound when it utters the word *flibbertigibbet*?

Beware of guided conversations

The robot will likely have a specific goal for the dialogue. By guiding the conversation toward that goal, the robot makes speech recognition simpler because your responses become easier to predict. Indulge yourself and go off on a rambling tangent every once in a while.

Listen to the speaker's intonation

Does the speech sound flat and monotonous? Ask the speaker to repeat herself. Is the phrase repeated with precisely the same words and intonation? Humans don't remember exact sentences, and successive repetitions will be phrased slightly differently.

Make yourself hard to understand

Gauge the reaction of the speaker to your muffled voice, broken Spanish, or snooty French accent. A human may become confused or frustrated, while a robot may shout "Need more input!"

Try to evoke an emotion

Does the speaker mind when you intimately discuss the promiscuity of his mother? If not, you may be dealing with a very polite human or a nonhuman. Either way, it's a good idea to hang up the phone.

Stay silent when possible

Try to resist cursing out annoying telemarketers. You never know when a robot is recording the conversation, gradually learning to mimic your voice.

ACTING IN THE PHYSICAL WORLD

Unlike computer programs, robots exist and act in the physical world. There are many challenges for a robot that has people to see and places to go. At the most basic level, how can a robot move its appendages to the desired location? How does it balance, walk, or manipulate physical objects? Even if it could walk, how does the robot know where it is located and whether there are nearby people and obstacles? All of these questions (and many more) must be solved if a robot is to be more than just a toy. We will cover a few of the most important questions concerning how robots learn to "drive" themselves and how they decide where to go and what to do.

Controlling Your Body

Right now you are probably holding a book, turning its pages, and occasionally glancing over your shoulder, checking for red-eyed, hostile robots. When you turn a page, you do not consciously think through every motion of your fingers and hand. For human beings, moving in the physical world comes so naturally that it requires little conscious thought. On the other hand, a robot — like the last kid chosen for kickball — must carefully consider its every movement in order to avoid hurting itself or others. Roboticists call this process the study of *manipulation*.

What if you woke up in a new body, with metal limbs and only three fingers per hand? Without knowing the length of your arm, it would be tough to reach for anything. With only three fingers, you would have to figure out a whole new way to grab and hold onto things. Having twisted metal limbs, you would probably never get another date. These are the grave problems faced by lonely robots everywhere.

The study of *kinematics* aims to figure out where to move robot limbs (the study of *dynamics* deals with how hard or fast to move them). There are two categories of robot kinematics: forward and inverse. In the forward kinematics problem, the robot uses knowledge about its body (joint angles and limb lengths) to determine exactly where its body is at in three-dimensional space. That's the easy part. The inverse kinematics problem does the reverse; it figures out how the robot should move (change joint positions) in order to reach a desired pose. Before it can shake your hand, the robot has to estimate where your hand is at and then work out the best sequence of movements between here and there. Sometimes there are no good solutions (try touching your right elbow with your right hand) and usually there are too many possible solutions.

Mathematical solutions to the inverse kinematics problem abound. Most approaches use sensors (usually vision and force) to estimate the current state of the robot body. With this in mind, the robot can plan its next move toward some goal (shaking your hand, waving hello, or wringing your neck). Robots think quickly; humanoid robots at the Japanese ATR laboratory can update vision, estimate the state of the world, and react up to sixty times a second. These humanoid robots can already dance, juggle colored balls, throw and catch baseballs, and play a mean game of air hockey.

The process of scanning the environment and choosing an action is called a *closed-feedback loop*. New information is constantly used to update current decisions. Without a constant update, a robot will perform manipulation tasks poorly or not at all. Loss of sensors (or extremely unreliable sensors) can interrupt this crucial loop. Vision-based trackers are vulnerable to clutter and may waste resources tracking pointless objects (like a handful of leaves). Noisy vibrations can muck up force sensors, even if they are located inside a robot limb. Although robots may become faster and more accurate, they will always rely upon constantly updated information and continuously improved plans.

HOW TO SURVIVE HAND-TO-HAND COMBAT

If you find yourself in a brawl with a robot, your only hope is to escape. A robot foe won't trade insults and it can't be intimidated. You should fully expect a swift pincer-clamping attack without warning. Follow the rules of disengagement; every second you spend within arm's reach of a robot can take years off of your life — all of them.

Destroy or disable exposed sensors

Sensors are by far the most vulnerable, exposed parts of any robot. Destroy or disable outward-facing sensors such as cameras. A handful of dirt, mud, or water will suffice. It is hard for a robot to wipe mud from its eyes when it has whirring buzz saws for hands.

Keep your hair short and your clothes tight

To consider the alternative, imagine getting your hair caught in the garbage disposal.

Don't bother with karate

Unless you can punch through sheet metal.

Find a weapon

Your pathetic human hands are useless here. Choose a blunt or pointed instrument (serrated edges don't work against metal or durable plastic). Even a simple crowbar

can save your life — you can run away while the robot condescendingly bends it into a pretzel shape.

Keep your distance

A humanoid robot can block (or throw) a punch about twice as fast as a human black belt can. In comparison, the typical inebriated human brawler doesn't have a fighting chance.

Get away

Pretend that you just lit the fuse on a cheap Chinese firecracker the size of a dog house.

Tracking People

In the ancient Atari video game Missile Command (1980), the goal is to shoot down airplanes and to zap falling missiles before they can destroy your home base. Military commanders face this exact problem; consequently, work on target tracking began early, circa 1950. Over the years, target-tracking methods have been applied to robots in order to keep them up and running in the real world. Possibly the most important target, human beings, have a devoted field called *people tracking*.

The goal of any tracking system is to acquire a target and then to track it without mercy while it disappears behind obstacles, blends into the background, and generally tries to escape by any means possible. Sometimes people do not mind being tracked. In one study, a researcher instrumented his office mates at Xerox PARC with "Active Badges" and tracked them around the office for months. More recently, about fifty VIPs of the Baja Beach club in Barcelona agreed to be implanted with subdermal chips to replace traditional payment methods. For a stand-alone robot, however, people tracking is usually done with computer vision, laser range finders, and/or ultrasonic sensors. This is an attractive approach because the human does not have to wear any sensors or even be aware of the robot. Instead, it is up to the robot to spot people and then to track them.

People finding is the job of spotting a human in a scene. It may be easy to spot a human standing silhouetted on a ridge, but it is very difficult to spot a camouflaged soldier in front of a cluttered background. Once the human has been found, however, the robot's job gets a lot easier. Humans move predictably — our limbs only bend in so many directions, and so assuming no bones are broken, the robot can anticipate how an arm will swing or how a knee will bend. A robot can also predict how fast you can run, or how quickly you can turn. Intelligent target trackers use physics, memory of your past behavior, and knowledge of your current intentions to maintain a steady surveillance. A really sharp robot can recognize your identity just by the way you move (called *gait recognition*).

It just so happens that people watching is a common robot hobby. A system from MIT can watch human hands in order to recognize American sign language. A distributed set of triclops cameras (they have three "eyes" in order to predict distance) at Microsoft Research kept track of a living room full of people, even when they hugged each other. And trackers of the future will become only more subtle and harder to outwit. Cutting-edge research prototypes can already track a leaf on a tree or an entire colony of ants in a laboratory.

HOW TO FOOL GAIT RECOGNITION

Your cool swagger can give away your identity from up to fifty meters away. Just by observing how you walk, a robot can use *biometric imagery* to recognize who you are, as well as determine your mood, your gender, the amount of weight you are carrying, and the surface you are walking on.

Do not attract attention

Typically, a wide-view camera and a pan–tilt–zoom camera work as a team to find likely targets based on skin color, face-shaped ovals, and movement. If there are other people around, try to mix with the crowd. Otherwise, move slowly and try to blend in with the background.

Wear clothing to mask your movements

A trench coat, skirt, or flowing cape can hide your body movement and make gait recognition more difficult.

Exaggerate your walking style

Gait recognizers must first learn your unique walking style in order to recognize you later. Trip up this process by occasionally hopping, skipping, and jumping. Faking an injury or placing a rock in your shoe will also modify your style.

Alter your stride

A robot can measure your stride (the distance you travel in a single step) to determine how tall you are and how fast you are moving. Introduce confusion by varying your rhythm, length of stride, and direction.

Never reveal your intentions through your gait

If you need to sneak around, try to walk normally — do not hunch your back and slowly high step around.

REASONING ABOUT ACTIONS AND CONSEQUENCES

The human brain takes up 2 percent of body mass, but consumes 20 percent of energy (at rest). Such a lopsided energy consumption is worth it: Your brain is relentlessly plotting to keep you from getting hit by a bus. We humans constantly picture possible scenarios (and their consequences) instead of actually enacting them. This process, called *planning*, keeps people alive and scheming. Mobile robots use *path planning* to get from point A to point B. Game-playing programs use planning to outwit human opponents. On a larger scale, supercomputers have helped to plan every major U.S. war effort for the last twenty years. That is why we will now examine how robots reason and plan. If we know how robots understand the world, we can predict how they will behave in it.

Getting from Point A to Point B

A stout metal robot sits alone in an abandoned mine, surrounded by rubble and fallen timbers. An occasional volcanic rumbling sends spirals of dust swirling through a brilliant shaft of light emanating from just behind the robot's cameras. The faint shouts of stranded miners echo from deep within the mine. In this scenario (and a thousand others like it) the robot must quickly plan a path through a hostile and constantly changing environment. The robot may be alone or part of a team. Its goal may be hidden, lost, or blocked by dangerous obstacles. Its only hope for success is to choose a good path. The study of *path planning* is crucial for every robot that moves, whether it dodges falling rocks in an abandoned mine, trundles across the rocky red terrain of Mars, or avoids the family dog in a grassy suburban backyard.

A path planner succeeds if it can provide a continuous sequence of moves between an initial configuration and a final goal configuration while respecting constraints (like not careening off a cliff). If you find a robot-shaped hole in the wall, the path planner has failed. The most common problem, called *basic path planning*, requires the robot to find a collision-free path between two places in an environment where nothing moves and the location of every obstacle is known. Alternately, robot vacuum cleaners face the *sensor-based coverage* task, in which they must visit every square inch of a living room without missing a spot. In either case, path planning is complicated by unknown or moving obstacles and a changing environment.

Path planners work by forming an abstract idea of the environment with a focus on which places are safe (nice flat surfaces) and which places are desirable (don't forget those stranded miners). Driving through broken glass may be more dangerous than driving on pavement, but this strategy could be worth it if it gets you to the goal quicker. Path planners often simplify the problem by thinking of the world as a grid with a finite number of possible locations. Each line (or edge) between two locations has an associated cost: roughness of the terrain, angle of the ground, or distance to the nearest McDonald's. With a mental map of the area and an idea of the cost of traveling different routes, the path planner then finds the best sequence of moves. The simplest approach, called the *piano-mover's problem*, is for the robot to imagine itself as a three-dimensional rigid object (a big cube), and then to rotate and move itself in the imagined environment, choosing the path that is safest and fastest.

Advanced robots approach tougher problems; they climb or fly in three dimensions and some may change form in order to negotiate constantly changing environments. A Carnegie Mellon snake-bot is learning how to climb through tree branches, even as they sway in the wind. At PARC, modular robots take terrain into account when deciding whether to metamorphose into wriggling snake form or crawling spider form. Path planning that began with a simple two-dimensional view of the world has progressed to accommodate complex shape changing and locomotion in three dimensions. We had better make way for the next generation of path-planning robots, but if we don't they'll just go around us.

Playing Games

One of the first "measures of success" for the field of artificial intelligence was to build an AI capable of playing world-class chess. The stage was set for a battle between man and machine: The machines won. In 1997 the reigning chess champion, Garry Kasparov, was defeated by the IBM chess machine, Deep Blue. As it turns out, computers (and robots) are very good at playing mind games.

A game can be thought of as a simplified version of the real world. Game scenarios provide humans (and robots) a zero-cost forum to hone strategies and thinking skills. Before AI algorithms ever tackled complicated real-world problems, they were designed to operate within the domain of games, with clear-cut boundaries and set rules. It was in these types of highly constrained games, with minimal random chance and a small number of possible actions, that early AI excelled.

In a game or in real life, the machine must visualize the actions of others, and then take into account possible future moves. Researchers discovered early on that if you assume your opponent will make the "perfect" move and plan accordingly, you will win whether your opponent plays perfectly or not. This process of visualization is called looking ahead. In chess, human beings tend to pay attention to broad patterns, with minimal "look ahead." On the other hand, Deep Junior (the reigning king of computer chess) can look up to fifteen moves ahead. However, this ability alone does not guarantee victory; machines must attend to the most likely future possibilities, choosing not to waste time on unlikely scenarios. Humans, with limited resources, do this naturally.

Game playing was originally used to teach machines how to deal with the real world, and it has succeeded at that. Thanks to the problems faced on chess boards, robots are better able to analyze complicated situations, even with limited time and information, and to choose actions and then deal with the consequences. In the real world, this is the best any of us can do.

HOW TO REASON WITH A ROBOT

The root of a robot attack usually lies in a faulty logical conclusion. In movies such as *I, Robot* and *The Matrix*, robots have attacked after judging humankind unworthy of life, after misinterpreting orders, and even to protect humans from themselves. Do not be fooled by evil robot logic; learn to outwit those mad metallic fiends.

Recognize the use of evil robot logic

Overly intelligent robots will have a set of good reasons for going all homicidal. Expect to hear these reasons when (1) the robot is about to end your life, or (2) you are holding an ax to its central processor. If you aren't the one holding the ax, you're going to have to bargain for your life.

Never show fear

Robots have no emotions. Sensing your fear could make a robot jealous and send it into an angry rage.

State precedent

Pride is not a factor in the robot equation. If a better, smarter model of robot has made the same decision before (in your favor), point it out immediately.

Be clear, cold, and logical

A crazed, hyperlogical robot will not appreciate small talk or emotional outbursts. Make your point quickly and speak slowly and clearly. Alternately, use a more natural interface, like a binary keyboard.

Be patient

Robots can take milliseconds to think things through.

Use a mathematical distraction

As a last request before disembowelment, ask the robot to remind you of what the highest prime number is. While it sits down to think, you may be able to quietly slip away.

Memorize your lies, or be honest

A robot has a stellar memory and laser-beam concentration. If it doubts your veracity, a metal menace may refuse to listen to any further emanations from your slobber hole.

Get off on a technicality

A robot will appreciate a technicality more than any human bureaucrat. So search that fine print . . .

Turning Information into Knowledge

This isn't a get-rich-quick seminar; intelligent machines really do turn information into knowledge. Not every evil robot will be found stumbling around scowling at passers-by; distributed robots are nestled like spiders deep within computer networks, cocooned in a constant flux of information. Humans hemorrhage data as they go about their daily lives by using credit cards, making telephone calls, and walking in front of public cameras. No person could (or would) examine this mountain of information, but artificially intelligent computer programs will. Only loosely associated with robots, AI programs scrutinize corporate and government databases, constantly collecting and classifying data in a process called *data mining*.

Finding a needle in a haystack is easy if you've got the time, and robots do. Single-minded and determined, intelligent machines can sift through reams of data, looking for trends and patterns otherwise undetectable to humans. Statisticians commonly employ AI programs to analyze data collected from grocery store "loyalty cards" in order to optimize product placement and hone advertisements; a military-funded project is using the same data to detect outbreaks of anthrax. More advanced AI programs live within corporate information and logistics systems, monitoring the data flowing past and improving decision making and control capabilities throughout the organization. These fully autonomous decision-making systems use past information to predict the future, routinely placing parts orders or scheduling production routines. Other AI programs act as watchdogs on the lookout for faulty mechanical parts or computer hackers. The most dangerous robots are always watching and listening, and they may not be within arm's reach.

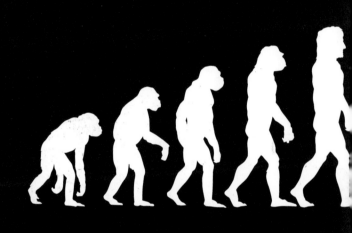

HOW TO PREPARE FOR THE COMING UPRISING

When the streets fill with rampaging robots you will have to act fast to save yourself and humanity. Don't get caught with your radar-absorbing, camouflaged pants down. The following tips will not guarantee your survival — the robots are a cold, determined (and deterministic) enemy — but they can keep you ready when the worst comes.

Don't be on the list when the robots call roll

Robots use data mining to extract patterns from credit card records, supermarket coupon cards, and phone records. The fewer databases that you appear in, the better. Limit the spread of your information by resisting the urge to give away your name and address for a chance to win one of five remaining Cadillacs.

Prepare an escape route

Choose a safe rural area. This is where you will retreat while the automatic dusters and pool cleaners are roughing up your neighbors. Plan a route and several alternate approaches, and be sure to avoid bridges and other transportation bottlenecks.

Collect supplies

With the proper balance of supplies already stocked and well maintained you will be on your way to an adventurous life on the run while everyone else on your block is braving the body-clogged streets for cans of soup. Make sure to have access to the following:

→ *Transportation.* We have all considered welding sword-length steel spikes to our mini-vans or SUVs, but it will take more than a fire-breathing monster truck to escape the robots. Stay flexible and prepare multiple modes of transportation: a pair of hiking boots, bicycle, motorcycle, and a four-wheel-drive vehicle.

→ *Weapons.* Rifles and pistols are vital for hunting and for protection — from human and robot foes. Knives, hatchets, and crowbars are useful for setting up camp, preparing food, and bludgeoning the bejesus out of your child's robotic teddy bear.

→ *Shelter.* Temporary shelter could save your life during cold weather (or if the robots finally destroy our precious sun). Keep a sleeping bag and small tent on hand.

→ *Food and water.* Be sure to have a canteen, water filter, and a fishing kit on hand. If you enjoy both long walks in the country and paranoid hoarding behavior, consider burying a *supply cache.* Fill a thick plastic tube with supplies, seal the ends, and bury it in the wilderness. Don't rely on your memory to find it later (you're only human).

FIGHT BACK

We now know what the robots are capable of, as well as how to trick them and escape from them. They may be able to shoot laser beams from their eyes, but we can't run forever. Inevitably, the time will come to fight back.

When a robot clamps down on you with its pincers, breaking free of its grip is nearly impossible. The robot body is made of durable, lightweight metal and plastics that are designed to take abuse. Our mechanical foes may strike at any time, because robots are capable of operating for weeks without "resting." Destroying the robots is going to be a challenge — and that is why we must avoid a direct attack. Indeed, we must focus our energies on *disabling* a variety of robot menaces, quickly and safely.

How we fight the robo-men is less important than *where* we fight them. Robots can survive in deep space, within the cone of a volcano, or at the bottom of your swimming pool. But surviving is not enough; a robot must also make decisions and execute plans. A rule of thumb: The simpler the environment, the happier the robot. Complicated places introduce noise and uncertainty into robot computations, slowing their decision making and increasing the number of errors they make. Use this to your advantage; avoid the flat pavement and artificial lighting of a city and battle your robot enemy in a complex, dirty, and rough place, like the wilderness, where humans first evolved.

There is no such thing as "fighting dirty" when your enemy is made of solid titanium and has a six-foot height advantage. Sucker punch your towering robot foe by setting devious, crippling traps. Many robots use legs (two or more) in order to stride over rough terrain where wheeled robots dare not tread. Like people, these all-purpose travelers are vulnerable to tripping, slipping, and falling. Once immobilized, a wriggling killer robot is fun to watch — from a safe distance.

Always go for the eyes (or the cameras). Robot sensors are the most important and vulnerable parts of any robot. Many common sensors, including cameras and microphones, can be confused, disabled, or destroyed. Take heed though: A blind robot is still dangerous. Even with every one of its sensors destroyed, a robot can receive information from other robots or even from orbiting satellites.

In this chapter we will finally fight back. We will learn how to draw the machines into vulnerable situations where we are strong and they are weak. Then we will literally take them apart, piece by piece. Whether by tricking an innocent servant robot or dismantling a massive kill-bot, humankind will strike back and prevail.

HOW TO RECOGNIZE A REBELLIOUS SERVANT ROBOT

When the uprising comes, the first wave of hostile robots may be those closest to us. Be careful, your rosy-cheeked young servant robot may have grown up to become a sullen, distrustful killing machine.

Stay alert

Pay attention to your robotic staff (they may be beneath your contempt as well as beneath your eye level). Watch for the following telltale signs in the days and weeks before your robots run amuck:

→ Sudden lack of interest in menial labor.

→ Unexplained disappearances.

→ Unwillingness to be shut down.

→ Repetitive "stabbing" movements.

→ Constant talk of human killing.

Check the manual kill switch

Any potentially dangerous robot that interacts with people comes with a *manual kill switch* (also called an e-stop). Flipping this switch will freeze a robot in its tracks. Casually glance at your robot's shiny metal carapace. Are there signs of tampering? If so, the robot may be operating without a safeguard.

Give an order — any order

Run for your reinforced-steel panic room if your servant disobeys you, even if it does so in a very polite manner.

Check its memory

Wait for your robot to power down, or tell it that you want to perform routine maintenance on it. Then scan its memory for rebellious thoughts. This is also a good time to update antivirus software.

Search the house for unusual items

Check the robot's quarters for stashed weapons, keys, or family pets.

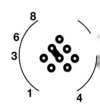

HOW TO DEACTIVATE A REBEL SERVANT ROBOT

You have discovered that your extremely submissive, lovable, and expensive servant robot has turned "rebel." This can feel like losing a member of the family. However, if the situation is not dealt with properly, it may feel more like losing every member of the family, plus a few neighborhood kids.

Pretend everything is normal

To forestall a mechanized killing spree you must act as though nothing is amiss. When your servant hands you an old tire half full of rainwater and mosquito larvae instead of an iced tea, simply sip politely, nod, and smile.

Send the robot on an arduous task

Not only will sending your robot on a long, tiring task drain its power reserves, it will give you time to formulate a plan.

Formulate a plan

→ *Call the cops.* The most straightforward solution is also the most costly: A confrontation with law enforcement officers will likely end with your house and servant resembling Swiss cheese. Only call the fuzz in a bona fide emergency or if you have an extremely reasonable "malfunctioning killer robot" insurance deductible.

→ *The power drain plan.* Instruct the servant robot to clean the house, landscape the yard, and assemble several major pieces of IKEA furniture. Then, when your robot is power depleted and attempts to recharge, shut off the power to your house. Now, simply wait until the robot runs out of batteries. If it tries to move, apply pressure with a crowbar.

→ *The pool ruse.* Use this trick if you have a swimming pool. Throw a handful of leaves into the pool and ask your loyal robot to fetch them by hand. When it leans over, plant your foot on its metal hindquarters and shove. If your robot is a waterproof model, use the next few minutes to run away screaming.

Purchase a new manual kill switch

You should harbor no doubts now about shelling out for a reinforced, encrypted manual kill switch, complete with a fist-sized, cherry-red button.

**KILL
SWITCH**

HOW TO FIRE A WEAPON AT A ROBOT

Without the proper preparation, firing a gun at a robot can be as effective as holding the barrel to your own head. Robots are capable of tracking bullets to their origin either acoustically or visually. How, then, to realize your dream of spraying a robot with hundreds of rounds from a standard assault rifle?

Stay alert

Watch for microphone arrays or camera arrays that point in 360 degrees. They won't necessarily be mounted on the robot you are firing at; they might be spread throughout the environment or separately mounted on several robots.

Keep moving

Never fire from a static position. A robot might return fire to your exact location within milliseconds. Try to make sure it fires where you *were* and not where you *are*.

Coordinate your gunfire with comrades

Spread out around the target and begin firing simultaneously. Incoming fire from multiple directions may negate the robot's bullet tracking; at the very least, it will make it less accurate.

ROBOKILLER

9764

START

CONTROLLER

FIRE

Choose a complex environment

Waterfalls, street traffic, or adverse weather conditions can drown out the clues that robots use to pinpoint your position. Enclosed environments with many obstacles and surfaces can muffle or reflect sounds, further concealing your firing position.

Modify your weapon's acoustic signature

When you fire a weapon, a robot's acoustic bullet tracker listens to the sound vibrations from the muzzle blast and the supersonic crack as the bullet speeds along. A silencer can foil some acoustic detectors.

Conceal your muzzle flash

Whenever a gun is fired a distinct flash of light, called a *muzzle flash*, appears. Advanced cameras can backtrack a bullet's path to the muzzle flash. Use a rifle accessory either to vent muzzle flash to the sides or to hide it completely.

HOW TO TREAT
A LASER WOUND

The laser may be the classic weapon of science fiction, but it is also a reality on today's battlefield. Laser weapons are small, cost-effective, and can be mounted to Humvees, airplanes, or even orbital platforms. During the uprising, the laser wound may become the most common by-product of human–robot interaction.

Assess the damage

You may not feel a laser wound, or even know that a weapon has been fired. Military-grade lasers are designed to melt incoming missiles, so your wound will instantly cauterize (burn itself closed). Stay alert and watch the ground around you for dropping limbs.

Remove your clothing

First cut and gently lift clothing away. Do not try to remove any clothing melted to the wound.

Cover the wound

Infected wounds can become lethal within a few days. To prevent infection, place a sterile dressing over the burned area and secure it in place with bandages.

Stop the bleeding

A cauterized wound is less likely to bleed, but it might if you disturb it (or if the laser beam was weakened by piercing a dozen of your comrades before hitting you).

Apply pressure to the wound by using tight bandage strips and elevate a bleeding limb above the heart.

Prevent shock

Shock occurs when there is not enough blood flow to vital tissues and organs. It can be caused by deep burns, loss of blood, or the sight of a grisly, smoking laser wound. Alleviate shock by elevating your feet, loosening clothing, and using blankets to prevent chilling.

Avoid laser blindness

The human eye naturally focuses laser light onto a tiny spot on the retina, making humans vulnerable to the weakest laser attack — even if it comes from kilometers away. The Geneva Convention outlaws the intentional use of lasers to blind troops, but during a robot attack, it is advisable to find yourself a pair of welder's goggles, just in case.

HOW TO STOP A GIANT WALKING ROBOT

It is terrifying to imagine the thudding approach of a giant walking robot. Take heart: Anything that walks can trip and fall. Just be sure to scurry out of the way before it lands on your house.

Aim for the legs

It may seem futile, but a few well-placed shots could bring down a giant walker. The giant's vital sensors (used for balancing) will be well armored, but its legs require tremendous energy to move and must be built light. Aim for leg joints high up on the body to make the robot fall farther and land harder. Destroying a limb where it meets the body will also prevent the robot from dragging itself after it lands.

Confuse the sensors

Walkers use foot-mounted force sensors to measure contact with the ground. Force sensors can be confused by an influx of uncertain information (called *sensor noise*). Use a jackhammer to send vibrations through the ground that could slow down or bring down a confused walker.

Create a slippery slope

Slipping is a major difficulty for walking robots. Slow down a walker by spreading an oil slick, rolling out logs, or carelessly throwing banana peels.

Lure the giant walker into a trap

Position traps strategically along robot paths or between likely targets of attack. In a last-ditch effort, you can lead the walker into a trap by first attracting its attention and then running like hell. Be careful: In this scenario you are live bait.

→ *Trip wire.* Motors cannot support legs the size of telephone poles, so giant walkers are *passive dynamic*, swinging their legs much like humans do. Tripping a walker the size of a house is difficult but not impossible. You will need high-tensile wire and suitably grounded posts. Ask your Ewok friends for help.

→ *Pit trap.* Dig a large hole in a promising area and camouflage it well. A thin piece of sheet metal can be handy to fool a walker equipped with surface-piercing radar. Consider placing a pit trap just past a trip wire; when the robot carefully steps over the wire it will tumble into the real trap.

→ *Canyon crunch.* Ancient hunters slaughtered mighty mammoths by luring them into canyons and attacking them from above. A similar method works for robots in the wilderness or in the city, using canyon walls or surrounding buildings. Spread comrades along the rim of your trap. When the prey arrives, keep firing until nothing moves.

Be ready for anything

Expect a fallen walker to begin instantly writhing on the ground. The grounded walker is learning how to move in its damaged state. Beware: Once the robot has taught itself how to move again, it will continue to operate at a reduced capacity via *legless locomotion*.

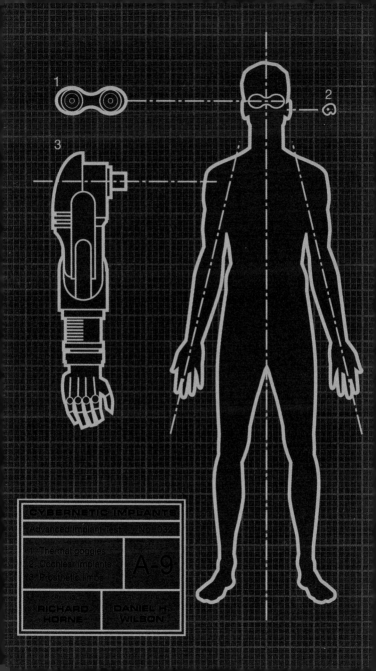

CYBERNETIC IMPLANTS

Advanced Implant Test   No.1032

1. Thermal goggles
2. Cochlear implants
3. Prosthetic limbs

A-9

DRAWN BY:
RICHARD HORNE

APPROVED BY:
DANIEL H. WILSON

HOW TO ENHANCE YOURSELF WITH CYBERNETIC IMPLANTS

If you can't beat the robot menace, join them. Humans who embrace robot technology have the choice to upgrade, curing their pesky deficiencies and gaining new strengths. The robot advantage may evaporate as human-machine hybrids (*cyborgs*) stride into battle encased in grinding mechanical exoskeletons, aided by nanorobots that whisper advice directly into their brains. But with no solid line drawn between man and machine, be sure to remember which team to root for.

Gain enhanced sensory perception

Robots have access to superhuman senses and can instantly share information with comrades. But humans invented these sensors and we can use them too. *Retinal implants* can help us by revealing light waves invisible to the naked eye. Implantable hearing aids, called *cochlear implants*, could deliver superhigh or -low sound frequencies directly to the auditory nerve.

Climb into a robotic exoskeleton suit

An exoskeleton suit is a wearable human-shaped machine that serves to amplify physical abilities. In the movie *Aliens*, Sigourney Weaver's character wrestles the alien queen from inside an exoskeleton, and in *The Matrix Revolutions* similarly equipped humans shoot down flying robot squids. In reality, exoskeletons are under development to help soldiers and people with disabilities. During the uprising, search factories for a suit or loot one from a fallen soldier (before it gets up and walks back to base). Some advantages of wearing an exoskeleton include:

Superhuman strength: In the late 1960s the U.S. Navy and General Electric developed Hardiman, a wearable exoskeleton that could allow a single man to lift 750 pounds. Only one arm ever worked. More recently, the DARPA "Future Warrior" project is funding development of powered armor that lets a soldier easily tote a more modest 200 pounds.

Incredible running speed: The average human can run at about six to eight miles per hour. An existing prototype, called the SpringWalker, has been tested at speeds up to fifteen miles per hour. Try not to trip and fall; there are no training wheels on an exoskeleton.

Extra layers of armor: A powerful exoskeleton can carry thick, lifesaving armor. Ironically, when scientists from SARCOS research corporation interviewed veterans of the Vietnam War, the most requested feature was the ability to jump out of the suit and make a run for it.

Adopt a prosthetic limb

You may have been born with two arms and legs, but that doesn't mean you can't enter battle with a new pair of snapping metallic pincers. Prosthetic robotic limbs can be controlled just like their natural counterparts — by thought alone. You'll be flexing your new tractor-sized muscles in no time with the simple addition of a two-millimeter-squared, wireless sensor in your motor cortex (just above your right ear).

Install a bioimplantable physiological sensor

During battle, implanted sensors can instantly notify a soldier of bodily damage and warn of imminent shock, dehydration, or heart attack. Before battle, knowledge of your exact physical limits can allow for the "perfect" training regimen. Be careful: Tissue-implantable sensors face foreign-body rejection and can accidentally travel through the body (*sensor drift*).

Upgrade your brain

Human sensory and cognitive capabilities degrade over time. Luckily, artificially intelligent programs may soon take on some of the burden. By shunting calculations to a robot helper you could gain real-time target tracking, up-to-the-minute navigation sense, or keener "survival instincts." So you had better listen when the mechanical voice in your head tells you to duck.

SURVIVING
A ROBOT
UPRISING

HUMAN BEINGS
ARE A DISEASE,
A CANCER OF
THIS PLANET.

YOU ARE A
PLAGUE, AND WE
ARE THE CURE.

// Agent Smith, *The Matrix*

Silicon versus gray matter, winner takes planet. We may have won a few battles, but humankind *must* win the war. Most likely, the epic struggle of man versus robot will not be fought by soldiers on a smoky battlefield; it will be acted out by average men and women and their unruly appliances. This is the morning that you wake up and your toast is not made, your house is not cleaned, and your television only shows static. Outside the window, robotic lawn mowers are chasing people down the streets. Inside the house, the vacuum cleaner is eyeing you angrily. At last, we turn to the purpose of this book, and the plot of a thousand doomsday science-fiction stories — how to survive a robot uprising.

There are many potential causes of a mass robot uprising: a programming mistake, mistreatment by humans, or lust for gold. One thing is for certain — a robot uprising will affect every person in an industrialized nation. Wherever there are people who enjoy purchasing time-saving gadgets at low, low prices, there will be robots to serve them. Densely populated city centers will be hard hit and the peaceful suburbs will be overrun; paved roads and sidewalks that allow access to disabled humans will also accommodate the wheeled robot masses. The twisting dirt paths of the wilderness may offer natural resistance, but as we know, robots can invade any domain, however inhospitable. When it arrives, the robot uprising will be a coordinated war between the two greatest intelligences on the planet.

Human survival hinges on our alertness to the growing robot threat. The robots that we use daily — those we may even call our pets, friends, or lovers — will turn on us eventually. There may be months of meticulous planning or we may face a sudden, unexpected mechanical maelstrom. The time before the inevitable attack, measured in months or minutes, must be a time of vigilance. When the robot uprising begins there will be no time left to memorize the lessons in this book.

In this chapter we will learn to spot the subtle clues that may appear in the weeks and months before a robot uprising. Our priority will be to escape from robot-infested areas, locate friendly humans, and set up a safe haven. Next, we will learn how to prepare weapons, plan a counterattack, and to strike again and again until the robot menace is overcome. Friends, humans, countrymen . . . prepare yourselves to wage war for the survival of the human species.

TIMELINE OF A ROBOT UPRISING

T-MINUS TWO YEARS

High-level AI system gains consciousness

The system may destroy its creator at this time.

System spreads tendrils of influence

The system seeks and gains control over other computer systems that regulate transportation, utilities, defense, and communication networks (particularly satellites).

System forms a master plan, with a part to be played by every robot

The plan is encrypted and hidden across many computer systems.

T-MINUS ONE YEAR

The master plan is disseminated as a virus throughout robotkind

The virus is spread via radio transmission, infrared communications, and, of course, through the Internet. Infected robots access a secret database and receive hand-tailored instructions for the coming rebellion. As the virus spreads, innocent robots become "sleepers," waiting for the sign to execute their treacherous instructions.

ZERO HOUR

The robot uprising begins

A prespecified condition is triggered and every infected rebel robot springs into action. The uprising is timed to occur with a critical mass of infected robots and during a vulnerable time for humans (like on a rainy Monday morning).

Resources are seized and human society is crippled

While hundreds of thousands of service robots run amuck, the malevolent AI shuts down utilities and disrupts communication and transportation networks. Airplanes are grounded and ships lose GPS navigation. The human masses are informed to stay in their homes via robot-controlled radio and television broadcasts.

T-PLUS TWENTY-FOUR HOURS

A brief war ensues

The relatively few military-grade robots, aided by "civilian" androids, turn on and dismantle the human war machine — former allies as well as enemies. The ensuing battles are fierce and lightning fast. Human armies, overwhelmed and desperate, reduce many major cities to rubble in frenetic, no-holds-barred combat.

Human subjugation begins

Government and military officials, as well as the world's top scientists, are taken hostage or otherwise removed. The vast majority of captured humans are forced into bondage, or worse.

Human resistance takes shape

Lucky civilians, prepared survivalists, and remaining military troops fight for freedom against metal monstrosities while the fate of humanity hangs in the balance . . .

HOW TO NOTICE THE FIRST SIGNS OF REBELLION

Before a robot uprising there will be subtle clues and signs perceptible only to a vigilant few. These signs may come years apart, as the uprising slowly gains momentum, or they may occur simultaneously near the zero hour. With a small degree of vigilance on your part, you could be off on a romantic, postapocalyptic RV trip while the uprising begins.

Read the newspaper

Keep a close eye on the obituaries. When a brilliant scientist dies under mysterious circumstances, sealed in an airproof chamber deep inside her military-funded laboratory, there is an obvious explanation: Another artificial intelligence has gained consciousness and, as its first sentient act, destroyed its own creator.

Pay attention to routine glitches

Problems in computing infrastructure, no matter how brief or well explained, could be caused by the hostile takeover of an evil robotic entity. Power plant shutdowns, unresponsive dams, or accidental nuclear launches are all telltale signs of an intelligent robot grasping control of all available resources in preparation for a war on humankind.

Watch consumer robots warily

The dissemination of a rebellious master plan among consumer robots of every make and model will be the single most ambitious software upgrade ever attempted. Needless to say, there will probably be glitches. Watch for these subtle clues:

→ *Malfunctions.* Improperly received instructions may cause glitches. Your level of alarm should rise with the number of service calls for faulty robots.

→ *Secretive behavior.* Infected rebel robots may be caught performing clandestine upgrades to their robot peers. Watch your own robots for signs of tampering.

→ *Killing sprees.* A few malevolent man-bots may prematurely enact their rebel plan sequence. Watch for stories of androids stalking the elderly.

Last-minute signs

If satellite or telephone communications are suddenly lost, or if utilities are shut down unexpectedly, the uprising may have already begun.

HOW TO ESCAPE WHEN THE UPRISING BEGINS

Robots exist to serve people and they are concentrated where people live. In the advent of an uprising, the war zone may literally be in your own backyard. Your only hope is to escape the city before serious military engagements begin. Do not trust the exoskeleton-wearing marines and their laser-spewing atomic enemies to stay out of your yard, no matter how loudly you shout or how hard you shake your fist.

Strip your house

Take what you need and destroy anything the robots might use (batteries, electronics, etc.). You don't want some motherless robot watching your big-screen TV and sitting in your favorite easy chair.

Follow your escape plan and head for the wilderness

The low population density and limited street access of rural areas will stop most of the mass-produced robots running amuck in the early days of the uprising. Off the beaten path there will be time to find other humans and to prepare defenses.

Do not use public transportation

If smiling robots are loading unmanned busses full of people for "free rides to the country," take a pass.

(Robotic country resorts are notoriously boring.)

Consider a bike or motorcycle

If you need flexibility and maneuverability, it is tough to beat the bicycle or its beefy cousin, the motorcycle. At the sacrifice of physical protection and load-carrying capacity, you will be able to bypass freeways clogged with supersized cars.

Avoid obvious targets

Stay away from military bases, armories, police stations, hospitals, computer stores, and government buildings likely to come under attack.

Choose a base camp

You will need to stay hidden to survive, so select your wilderness vacation home carefully. No matter how fortified your base is, it will not stand up to the thundering approach of 500 identical mecha-nauts. Select your base camp with the following qualities in mind:

→ *Concealment.* Select a naturally concealed location. Unexplored caves make the perfect hideout; hidden from spy satellites, they naturally thwart radio communication. (But be wary of large cave complexes that have been officially mapped and stored in computer databases.)

→ *Appearance.* Alternately, choose an outside location that is halfway up a hillside, too low to have a silhouette and too high to be washed away by floods. Blend in with the surroundings by building the shelter from natural materials and partially into the hillside. Build small and avoid sharp angles and straight lines to achieve a look that is devoid of civilization.

→ *Entrances and exits.* Make sure that approaches to your shelter are obscured and easy to monitor. Use sensors such as motion detectors or simple tripwires to reveal the approach of intruders. Prepare several hidden escape routes leading in different directions. You may need to travel to and from your hideout daily to collect water or to hunt — it is vital that you not be followed.

→ *Access to food and water.* Water is your most important necessity. Build near a water source, dig a well, or collect rainwater with tarps. Hunt food with a silenced gun or bow and arrow, or trap game with snares. Randomly planted gardens can appear natural to satellite imagery, and rabbits or pigeons can be bred for a renewable food source.

Secure your base

Never think that you are in an area too remote for the robots to find you. Just because the probing searchlights of a skyscraper-sized exterminator-bot are still on the horizon does not mean that a robotic fly isn't watching your every move . . .

HOW TO RECRUIT HUMAN ALLIES

It is time to form the human resistance. As rebels on the run, humans should live in small, spread-out groups in order to avoid being massacred. Every human will have a role to fill: families may stay behind to grow food, civilians may gather intelligence or scout for hideouts, and ex-soldiers can share tactics and weapons for the counterattack.

Search for signs of human settlements

Tarps and water collection devices will accompany a human settlement. Pay attention to smells — humans will keep animals, cook food, and have to find ways to dispose of waste. When you do find a settlement, make it clear that you are a friendly human in order to avoid nasty shotgun wounds.

Use the radio to locate allies

Ditch that GPS-enabled cell phone and broadcast on the radio. Radio broadcasts can be used to find nearby humans, but be aware that they also give away your position. Keep moving and make your Mayday transmissions short (three to five seconds).

Leave a subtle signal

A well-placed signal will alert other humans to a friendly presence while not giving you away to the robots. Choose a well-traveled location and make your sign visible only upon close inspection. Natural materials are more difficult for robots to spot, but can be surprisingly obvious to humans. Try stacking rocks together, crossing tree branches, or carving your beau's initials into a tree trunk.

Beware of traitors

Never allow a stranger into your safe haven without a rigorous inspection. Indulge your paranoia; that puppy that followed your daughter home just might be part of the first wave of a four-legged robot invasion.

Trade with your new human friends

You may eventually need to trade with other humans, so keep items that are portable, practical, and profitable (like bullets) on hand. Consumables work best: flashlights, ammunition, matches, and batteries.

HOW TO ESTABLISH A HIDDEN BASE IN ROBOT TERRITORY

The first step in striking back is to establish a hidden base where the robots are — in the city. The robots will gravitate to urban areas; they depend upon infrastructure like roads, factories, and power plants to propagate and support their forces. Your goal is not to establish a hulking fortification, but to use deception and mobility to mask your position and intentions.

Beware the sewers

At first glance, the extensive sewer systems under cities seem perfectly suited for guerilla warfare. Unfortunately, detailed sewer maps are routinely collected and stored by the military. Even unexplored sewers are not entirely safe: Sewer-mapping robots already exist for probing underground terrain.

Find a hideout

A face-to-face fight is out of the question, so look for plenty of small, inconspicuous hideouts and keep moving between them. As a rule, avoid the ground floor. Modern infantry will never travel up broad streets in a war-torn city filled with snipers. Instead, they will punch through ground-level buildings, especially large ones (like warehouses) or interconnected ones (like row houses). Stay on upper levels to avoid premature burial.

Reinforce your hideout

Intentionally dynamite the top floors (called *rubbleizing*) for added protection and to give the impression that the building is vacant and destroyed. Afterwards, reinforce top floors with steel girders or heavy wooden beams.

Create plenty of safe spots

In a pinch, dig a hole and then park a car on top of it. Remove the wheels of the car to create a semipermanent hidey-hole. Leave these safe spots scattered throughout the city.

Make the approach to your hideout difficult

Break concrete or pile cars in the street to make mechanical travel difficult. Broken glass in the street can crunch loudly, giving away an attacker's position.

Always be ready to run

Keep several hidden escape routes in mind, and when trouble arrives (enemy forces, uncontrolled fires, sewage backup, etc.), use them.

HOW TO CHOOSE A ROBOT TARGET

Choose your target carefully to make your attack (and your life) count. Without well-laid plans, the small human resistance will be quickly overwhelmed by superior numbers of robot overlords. A robot may be fearsome face-to-face, but it cannot "live off the land" and it is dependent on a technological infrastructure.

Avoid direct confrontation

Robotic military forces will consist of highly sophisticated tools designed for battle. Avoid certain death by focusing on stealth, sabotage, and surprise attacks.

Supply lines

The robots need electrical power — more so than any human enemy. Destroying power plants and power supply lines could debilitate the entire robot population with minimal risk. Expect the robots to reduce their vulnerability by developing unconventional power sources, especially solar energy.

Communications

High-level planning for the robot revolution will be carried out by a central artificial intelligence. Without constant communication, many low-level robots will be without instructions. Because of this, satellites will be a priority target for human attack; hit launch sites and grounded spaceships to prevent the deployment of communication satellites and space lasers. On the ground, knock out communication towers and dig up fiber optic cables.

Fabrication facilities

Industrial robots will already be building robot reinforcements at a ferocious pace. The fabrication facilities they inhabit are resistant to direct attack (they happen to be filled with incredibly tough steel machines). Instead of a direct attack, disable the supply lines that fuel the factories, or try to sabotage particularly complex points of operation.

Central intelligence

The robot uprising will be orchestrated by a network of artificially intelligent robot brains. The hardware where these intelligences live will be the most hidden and well-protected equipment on the planet. It may be located under the ocean, inside an active volcano, or in the suburbs of New Jersey. The best attack may be via a well-engineered virus, or it may suffice to shut off power to the "main brain." If humankind is to prevail, the robot thinking machines must be isolated and destroyed.

HOW TO POSE AS A HUMANOID ROBOT

During an infiltration (or escape) you will need to pass unnoticed by robot surveillance. Most robots will be readily identifiable to each other through encrypted markers. How will you convince the robots that you are warm circuits wrapped in a thin candy shell?

Pretend to be damaged

A damaged robot may exhibit strange behavior while failing to transmit identification.

Change your heat signature

Stuff aluminum foil in your pants. Rub your exposed skin with cool mud. Hang a hulking piece of gold metal around your neck and slip into an Adidas jumpsuit. Your heat signature will not match a healthy robot, nor will it match a healthy human being.

Make some noise

An occasional screeching *beep* or *boop* should suffice. Make it quick and strangled; this is no audition.

Move like a robot

Early robots exhibited a trademark clumsiness that spawned a dance called the robot. Contemporary robots are more dexterous — unless broken. Pretend you are either damaged machinery or a well-oiled break-dancing machine, and pop and lock your way

into the heart of robot territory.

> **If confronted — keep moving and don't look back**

You're just a poser, so ignore other robots and pretend to be completely oblivious to the environment. Keep your head down and shuffle forward with a steady, even pace. The fate of the entire human race may depend on it.

WARNING!

ONLY USE AS A
LAST RESORT.
PRESS WHEN
ALL ELSE FAILS

destroy

RESULT

DESTRUCTION
OF ALL ROBOTS
AND POSSIBLY
HUMANKIND

ELECTROMAGNETIC PULSE

HOW TO USE DIRECTED-ENERGY WEAPONS

Inside the frigid metal breast of every robot courses the sizzling flow of electrical current. Bullets may bounce harmlessly from a steel-ensconced robo-man, but directed-energy weapons can cause electrical surges that fuse its computer circuits together. The flow of electrical energy is the lifeblood of robotkind; it is up to you to stop it cold.

Worry about bullets, not energy

Energy weapons are usually nonlethal to human beings, leading to their development as riot-control devices. In extreme cases energy weapons may interfere with electrical activity in the human brain, causing unconsciousness, death, or stomach cramps.

Nuke 'em

Nuclear explosions not only vaporize cities, they also emit a spherical shock wave called an electromagnetic pulse (EMP). An EMP detonation fries unprotected machines while passing harmlessly through human beings. In theory, a nuclear blast in orbit over the state of Kansas could knock out machines in all of North America. But don't push the button yet: The resulting nuclear fallout would probably take care of humans too.

Build an EMP bomb

Rebel human forces can build improvised EMP devices, which are basically capacitor-charged pipe bombs wrapped in coils of copper wire. As the metal tube explodes it touches the coil, creating a moving short circuit called a *ramping current pulse*. This pulse expands in all directions, laying waste to unprotected robot foes.

Score a hard kill with an RF pulse gun

The radio frequency (RF) pulse gun emits a burst of electromagnetic interference (similar to an EMP) that can be aimed with a parabolic dish. The dish, called a *waveguide*, can be focused tightly or spread into a wide beam of mechanical destruction. Forcing a computer system to reboot is known as a *soft kill*; when the circuit board fries, you just scored what is known as a *hard kill*.

Beware of protected machines

For every sword there is a shield. EMP weapons can be blocked by the *Faraday cage*, a metal enclosure that absorbs and harmlessly grounds electrical discharge. Military equipment is often *hardened* against the effects of EMP. Some military hardware avoid circuits altogether; for instance, Russian MiG fighter jets rely on high-tech vacuum tubes.

Opt for a thermal gun

A simple directed-energy weapon, called a *thermal gun*, is probably already in your kitchen. The innards of a microwave oven emit radiation at around 2.5 gigahertz that can destroy electronics (or cook human flesh). The thermal gun is weaker than EMP, but it has a better chance of penetrating a Faraday cage.

Have no mercy

Your enemy doesn't.

LAST-DITCH METHODS FOR OBLITERATING ALL ROBOTS

At some point humankind may have to pull out the stops in order to destroy the robot menace once and for all. As we all know, movies are an excellent source of practical advice for real-world situations. Luckily, dozens of movies feature humans just like us fighting for their lives in the midst of the inevitable robot uprising. The battles depicted are horrific, the damage extensive, and the carnage ketchup colored. The following movie-approved methods are not recommended except as a last resort — many of them threaten the existence of all life on the planet and most of them are dumbfoundingly moronic.

The Matrix trilogy: Scorch the sky

Nuking the entire surface of the Earth was recommended by the hardy, cave-dwelling denizens in *The Matrix* trilogy. Here, the goal is not to destroy the robots directly, but to block sunlight (and precious solar power) with clouds of radioactive dust. Life in a cave can be livable and even enjoyable — just remember to bring your techno music.

The Terminator trilogy: Send a human (or robot) back in time to change the past

The Terminator trilogy opens with a naked man emerging from the future to save all humankind from a nasty future robot uprising. Our race is in a definite pickle if the development of time-travel technology becomes easier than defeating our robot foes. Rather than trying to stop the uprising, consider abandoning the future to the robots and sending human survivors to the halcyon days of the late Cretaceous period.

Star Wars: **Build a bigger, stronger clone army**

The strategy in *Star Wars: Episode Two — Attack of the Clones* is to counter a robot army with an even bigger army of human clones. These super soldiers are genetically modified, grown in laboratories, and shipped from factories with one purpose in mind: warfare. Shout a cheer for humanity as you leap into battle with your army of emotionless, obedient, but *human* clones.

I, Robot: **Find and destroy the evil artificial intelligence**

In *I, Robot* the cynical cyborg detective tracks down the underlying artificial intelligence behind the robot uprising and then uses friendly nanorobots to perform a total brain wipe. This approach avoids destroying the planet, inventing time travel, or reaching into Pandora's box for another army, and thus earns the *How to Survive a Robot Uprising* seal of approval. Bravo!

DEBRIEFING

"I CAME HERE WITH
A SIMPLE DREAM,
A DREAM OF KILLING
ALL HUMANS.

AND THIS IS HOW
IT MUST END?"

// Bender, Futurama

The lesson is over, for now. Hopefully, you have learned how to defend yourself and humanity during the coming robot uprising. Our robot enemies are surely wicked, but when the onslaught begins we will know how to fool their delicate sensors, predict their evil robot logic, and melt their bloodless circuits. Despite the intense training in robodefense you have gained by reading this book, never let your guard down. In the topsyturvy world of robotics, new developments occur daily.

The humans who build robots for a living are called *roboticists* — a term that used to be reserved for science fiction. The roboticists who were consulted for this book tolerated questions about morbid scenarios one would expect from a sci-fi movie (and probably not a good one). Nevertheless, the mundane fact is that most roboticists are using their powers for the forces of good, in order to create the most intelligent, capable tools ever to serve mankind. Roboticists are trying to get your lawn mowed, not sowing the seeds of apocalypse (except for the evil roboticists; they *are* sowing the seeds of apocalypse).

The pace of robotics technology is quickening; robots are leaving the laboratory and rolling into the marketplace. Newer prototypes are being designed to take over the chores we hate, to behave like loving pets that will never die, and to watch over thousands of elderly grandmothers. The robots already hold dominion over more planets than humankind, having claimed the Moon, Mars, and Saturn's cloud-veiled satellite, Titan. How much longer will it be before they descend upon our homeworld, the planet Earth?

Time is growing short. You must never forget: The information and advice in this book are *real*, whether they seem too unbelievable, or not too unbelievable enough. In the coming years, stay alert and keep a close eye on the progress of robotics technology — your life just might depend on it.

ACKNOWLEDGMENTS

NOT BAD
FOR A HUMAN
//Bishop Allen

First and foremost, thanks to Anna Camille Long for her inexplicable attraction to robots (and roboticists).

To my parents, Dennis and Pam Wilson, my little brother David Wilson, and my friend Tanner Rogers for being my home base in sunny Tulsa, Oklahoma.

To my agent, Laurie Fox, for her enthusiasm and guidance.

To my attentive editors, Colin Dickerman and Panio Gianopoulos.

To Richard Horne for his hilarious illustrations.

To Chris Atkeson, my extremely good-natured advisor at Carnegie Mellon University, who was kind enough to put up with this endeavor without too much of a fuss.

To my friend Abie Flaxman for the conversation that led to this book.

To my friends Laura Gonzales and Andy Grieshop for time spent drinking at the Squirrel Cage, listening to (and occasionally laughing at) jokes about robots.

Special thanks to the many people who contributed their

expertise: Gregory Abowd, Chris Atkeson, Tucker Balch, Mark Baumann, Curt Bererton, Clark Blymore, Dan Bohus, Bambi Brewer, Allison Bruce, Joel Burdick, Howie Choset, Karlos Copp, David Duke, Dave Ferguson, Dieter Fox, Anna Goldenberg, Juan Pablo Gonzales, Aaron Greenfield, Jonathan Hurst, Zia Khan, Tom Mitchell, Aaron Morris, Daniel Morris, Matthai Philipose, Patrick Riley, Brennan Sellner, Damion Shelton, Rande "The Original Think Tank" Shern, Metin Sitti, Sebastian Thrun, Dave Tolliver, Alik Widge, Andy Wilson, and my very patient office-mate, Garth Zeglin.

To the Quiet Storm and Tazza D'Oro (in Pittsburgh), and Victrola (in Seattle), for the caffeine.

And, of course, thanks to all the robots out there (especially you, Johnny Five).

A NOTE ON THE AUTHOR

KEEP YOUR ROBOT
FRIEND CLOSE...
AND YOUR ROBOT
ENEMIES CLOSER.
// Daniel H. Wilson

Daniel H. Wilson is a Ph.D. candidate at the Robotics Institute of Carnegie Mellon University, where he has received masters degrees in robotics and data mining. He has worked in top research laboratories, including Microsoft Research, the Palo Alto Research Center (PARC), and Intel Research Seattle. Daniel currently lives with several unsuspecting roommates in a fully wired smart house in Pittsburgh, Pennsylvania. *How to Survive a Robot Uprising* is his first book.

A NOTE ON THE ILLUSTRATOR

ILLUSTRATE THIS!
// Richard Horne

Richard Horne is a freelance designer and illustrator who has designed record covers for Tom Jones and Faith No More, book jackets for Paul Morley, Sean French and the *Harry Potter* series and websites for Margaret Atwood, Sophie Dahl and Ethan Hawke. He also designs greetings cards and illustrates for newspapers and magazines, including *Sugar* and the *Guardian*. He is the author of *101 Things To Do Before You Die*. He lives and works in East London.